Gail Thackray's

SPIRITUAL JOURNEYS

Visiting
John of God

Indian Springs Publishing

Printed in the United States of America.

Thackray, Gail
Gail Thackray's Spiritual Journeys:
Visiting John of God / by Gail Thackray

ISBN-13: 978-0-9848440-2-9
ISBN-10: 0984844023

Project Editor, Mara Krausz.
Cover design and layout conception by Teagarden Designs.
Copy editing by Kathy Glass.
Main front cover and back cover photographs by Mara Krausz.
Triangle graphic designed by Teagarden Designs.
Graphic on page 229 designed by Leah Feria Ordonia.
Page layout and design finishing by Lynn M. Snyder, Nosy Rosy Designs.

Published by
Indian Springs Publishing
P.O. Box 286
La Cañada, CA 91012
www.indianspringspublishing.com

*Words cannot suffice to express my gratitude
to Medium João (John of God) and the beautiful
benevolent spirits that work through him at the Casa.
With deepest appreciation for opening my heart,
for the guidance, and for the love that was
not only given to me but that he gives selflessly
everyday to anyone who asks.*

Table of Contents

CHAPTER 1

Flashback

I FIRST MET BUNNY at my "Cutting Psychic Cords" workshop. Bunny knew I was an animal communicator as well as a psychic, and she brought pictures of her dog Annie. Annie was not an old dog but she was having bad hip pain. Her run included a skip where she wouldn't touch the ground with the right back paw. As soon as I tuned in, I knew to ask about "dad," Bunny's husband Rick. This came as no surprise, since our health issues are often reflected in our pets. Sure enough, Rick had a right hip issue as well. In fact, it was so bad that at that very moment, he was lying down in the back of their camper while he waited for Bunny to finish the workshop.

I asked Bunny to bring Rick in. He could barely walk. He came in hobbling, doubled over in pain. He was sweating profusely and breathing heavily, like my request to have him come in was almost too much. Instinctively, I placed my hands lightly over his hip, sensing the energy. I was strangely transformed back in time to a vision of what appeared to be medieval England or northern France.

I found myself at the edge of an open field on a brisk winter morning. It was just past dawn and the field was moist with the early morning dew. A heavy uncomfortable feeling hung in the air. Then I realized I was in the midst of a battle. For the moment all was quiet, broken only by the exaggerated sounds of my heavy breathing and pounding heart. Anxiously anticipating, I waited for any movement. I was miserably uncomfortable, wearing heavy linen, well padded but soiled and wet. The clothing was held together by a thick leather belt from which hung several objects made of iron. In my left hand I held a makeshift bent metal shield, and in my right, a small but well sharpened deadly knife.

There seemed to be a pause, a moment of relief to catch my breath. Then out of nowhere, a gruff roar and a clank of iron rushed from the trees behind me. Before I had time to even turn around, I was hit. Incredibly excruciating pain in my lower back and hip brought me to my knees. I was hit by some kind of blunt metal instrument, like a ball with spikes. I'm now on the ground writhing in pain, not dead but wishing I were. Out of breath and losing consciousness, I am fighting desperately to stay on one knee as if I am prepared to fight back, but my adversary is gone. I am all alone.

Although I am experiencing this through Rick, I have no emotion. I do not actually feel any pain, but I am aware of excruciating pain. I do not feel anger and despair, but I am aware that I have these emotions to the deepest core.

I sense that Rick's father in his current life was somehow a player in this long-ago scene. I don't know his role exactly, but coming back to present time for a moment, I ask Rick to send love to his father. Rick rolls his eyes in acknowledgement that he knew somehow his dad would come up in all of this.

I then went to work psychically removing the remnants of this deadly ball. It looked like it had been made from leftover nails off the blacksmith's floor, now rusted and embedded in Rick's back. It was overgrown by an invisible network of thick rubbery cobwebs formed around his right hip and lower back. I envisioned cutting them away from Rick and his adversary, there on the battlefield in some long-gone time.

When I was done, I asked Rick to try to stand up. Then an amazing thing happened. He rose timidly, expecting the familiar pain, but he felt none. He rose a little at a time, straighter and straighter, checking his pain level each time, confused. An amazed smile gradually appeared over his face as he slowly realized that he could straighten without feeling any pain. The next thing we all saw was Rick standing completely erect, grinning like a Cheshire cat. He was standing up straight for the first time in many years! He started to take a few tentative steps. He couldn't believe it. He could walk! Upright and without pain! He told everyone watching in amazement how unbelievable this was. He made it back to his chair beside Bunny and sat down beaming, thrilled by what is normal to most, being able to sit on a chair without pain. I left him in bewildered happiness. I did several "cutting cords" sessions that night, some equally as miraculous.

This is what I loved, this is what I lived for! Each time I helped people in their healing was a tremendous high for me. I absolutely loved this process and felt blessed to be a part of it. What was I doing exactly? How was I getting this? I had learned how to feel and cut psychic cords in advanced Reiki. In fact, I was now a Reiki Master, teaching these techniques to my own students. However, it was more than that. Six years earlier, I had discovered quite by chance that I could talk to people's loved ones in spirit on the other side. This had been a mind-blowing revelation for me, and I had spent several years in disbelief. I was now at the point that I could admit it was happening, and I had found a purpose in this newly dispensed gift. I was certainly using my mediumship skills, intuition, and psychic senses, but the healing work involved more than this.

Visions of past lives, which didn't seem required for the healing, often spontaneously showed up. This was far beyond anything I'd ever read in any Reiki book. Way off the page. This was more than could be explained. When I did healings, I was following my guidance, following spirits who directed me. Still, I remained as baffled as anyone else.

I knew certain spirits had been aligned with me through the Reiki process, and beautiful benevolent spirits were using me as a physical means to provide their healing work. I also knew I had picked up additional guides and special energies from the different spiritual places I had traveled. I had visited several great masters, and some of what they had taught me was being incorporated into my "work." I had felt the presence of the Virgin Mary and smelled her rose scent while filming a sacred Icon that weeps myrrh oil. I had connected with higher guides from the Pleiades at a ranch in Washington. In many places in the world, I had felt the touch of beautiful spirits.

I knew I was blessed to be working with higher guides in spirit. I was not doing the healing myself. It is not as if I have some magic gift or touch to heal people. I know it was not me. Nor was I channeling *per se*. That is, I was not unconscious and allowing spirits to take over my physical body, although some details of what I said during healings seem clouded or fuzzy and often I could not recall them later.

What exactly I was doing, I was not sure. I could see people's relatives in spirit around them, which would often give them hope and peace. I could sometimes see their past lives and their physical and emotional ailments. All these things seemed to interconnect. I believed in a Divine Being or God, more so now than ever; the energy I felt left me knowing that this must in fact be the workings of some glorious Divine Source. I knew also that when the person could forgive and love, the healing was easier and more complete. Therefore the healing that was taking place had to be a connection between the people themselves and God.

I did not seem to have control over a session, and the results were often not what I would expect. I could not summon certain spirits to appear; I couldn't ask for specific results. I was discovering and learning myself, still on my own spiritual journey, and so far I had learned to say what I was sensing, no matter how weird or wild it seemed.

Two days later I got a call from an ecstatic Bunny. She could barely hold her excitement as she talked about how her husband was miraculously healed.

"It's as if he never had a problem. Years and years of being in pain and having had multiple surgeries and now he's walking like he never had a problem. It's a miracle!" She went on in disbelief,

"And you'll never guess. Annie, our dog is completely healed too! She's bouncing around like a young pup. The two of them were out walking today and she's been running around completely normal. She is completely healed too!"

I gave a little thank you to spirit. Of course, no matter how many times I would say, "It's not me, thank the spirits, and thank God," clients still tried to give me credit. I knew I wasn't doing these healings—I was just somehow part of the connection. Though for me, when I heard these stories of healing, it felt wonderful. This felt like my life purpose to help people in whatever capacity was mine.

A week later Bunny called again. This time the news was not so good. After the third day, Rick had slowly started to regress and his hip had gotten worse and worse until by the seventh day he was back to the same terrible state I had first seen him in. Annie's run had also gone back to the odd familiar skip.

"Could Rick come back and could you fix them again?" she pleaded.

"I would be happy to try," I said, but I knew some work had to be done by Rick as well.

By this point, I had cut back drastically from private readings and was concentrating on group workshops and events. I wanted to touch more people and felt that bigger groups would accomplish this. I wanted to teach people to connect to the energy themselves, learn the tools such as Reiki, meditation, and prayer, and realize how they could take control of their own lives.

Private readings drained my energy and left me feeling physically exhausted. I found there is a certain realm of spaciness that comes with mediumship and spiritual healing. Living too strongly and too much in that world caused the spaciness to spill over into my day-to-day life. For my own sanity, I decided to cut down the time and energy I had been exerting on private readings and to concentrate on using my gift to help teach others.

When doing private readings, I found that people were quite happy to completely turn their lives over to me, wanting me to direct their every move. No matter what encouragement I gave them, they thought that I must have more insight than them and could run their life better. I didn't want to be a psychic hotline to the other side. I had been given a little taste of the guru status. On the one side it might seem glamorous and could potentially be very profitable, but there was a definite downside. For people to anoint me a "healer," I was certainly not deserving of this title. I had my own life issues, my own human frailties, and by no means was I any kind of angel. I had lived a pretty adventurous full life, which had occasionally taken me down some not so innocent paths. I was not anyone's role model and I had not been chosen to be anyone's guru, I was sure of that.

So how could I empower others to take control of their own lives, their health, their emotional issues, permanently and confidently, doing it themselves?

Rick and Bunny continued to come to many workshops and events such as Reiki, Mediumship, and "How to Communicate with Animals." Many times, Rick would volunteer and get a tune-up. Each time the effects would last for about three days before he was back to square one. What was the purpose here? Surely there was something more. Clearly some kind of an energy adjustment was taking place. With the aid of spirit, Rick had aligned his energy and healing was done. However, when he left and he went back to his old patterns or negative thinking returned, the negative energy returned. I struggled internally with the desire to help people, but the greater desire was to teach them to be able to remain in a healed state by their own hand.

What were the experiences of other people I worked on? Sometimes the healing seemed to be a permanent adjustment that appeared to fix their problems. But sometimes, like with Rick, it was only temporary. What was going on here? I believed that there was a certain connection or adjustment that needed to be made by the person. They needed to open up, allow, and be involved in their own healing. However, if the person returned to their same thinking, their same lifestyle that caused these issues, pretty soon their ailment would return.

How could I help people connect with the energy of Divine Source permanently and continuously? Perhaps my next adventure would bring me closer to an answer.

CHAPTER 2

Getting Nudged to Brazil

IT HAS BEEN about six years since my spiritual journey began. Having finally accepted my role as a medium, I had learned to go with the flow. Unusual events became the norm. I had spent years questioning my gifts, ones that the old mainstream me would have had a more comfortable time passing off as simply an active imagination. Yet I had proven to myself, time and time again, that the uncanny details I was given must be from some otherworldly source. You see, it wasn't like I was your "usual" psychic that had been born clairvoyantly gifted. Rather, this "gift" had been bestowed on me at the ripe old age of forty. I found myself asking, "What is the purpose in all of this?"

I had been quite a successful businesswoman when I was suddenly thrown into this whole woo-woo world, one generally lived in by artsy sensitive types, whom I viewed as very different from me. Things that I would have simply not believed if they had happened to someone else started to happen to me. Talking to "dead people" had of course been one of those major milestones. Discovering that I could jump inside an animal and describe their every wish would have seemed impossible, yet this was revealed as a normal extension of my mediumship. Passing healing energy through the touch of

Reiki could have been a great purpose in life in itself, but somehow that was just the tip of the iceberg for me. Despite myself, I had become somewhat sensitive to energies enabling me to be empathic and to help people on a deep level. But more so, I was experiencing tremendous satisfaction from helping others connect to their loved ones and their inner selves.

No longer fighting these life changes, I embraced my spiritual side and decided to make this my life path and career. My husband, who had met and fallen in love with the other me, was having a difficult time with my new life purpose. I had always been a business-minded career woman concerned, like him, with the achievement of success, money, and all the trappings that came with it. Now, more content in the enjoyment of life, my highs came from helping people with their healing process.

I was convinced that if *I* could be psychic and see, hear, and feel things on a spiritual level, then anyone could. I wanted to deliver the message that "Everyone can do this!" I thought I had already arrived at my life's purpose, but it had only just begun....

There have been certain milestones in my psychic development, all of which came uninvited and out of left field, but none so obvious and profound as my journey to see John of God.

I had heard the name "John of God" pop up several times in connection with his reputation as a miraculous healer from Brazil who channels spirits that diagnose and do spiritual surgery on people.

In fact, this door kept opening and the way kept being presented to me. Clients I met talked about this great healer, magazine articles magically seemed to appear to me—all little coincidences and experiences that the other side uses to gently nudge us. *"Um, very interesting, would love to meet this man one day,"* I would think, but always with the reservation that I didn't have a life-threatening disease and so there was no urgent reason to go. Of course, I would always quickly clarify to my spirit guides listening that I didn't want that necessity to go, just in case they were thinking of giving me some medical crisis as a motive. It was just with mere curiosity that I contemplated a visit. Especially now since I was at the point where I could finally own up to being a Reiki Master and perhaps even deserve the titles "Healer" and "Medium." Yet there was a deep yearning inside me that knew somehow a visit to this special place in Brazil might bring me the spiritual answers I had been looking for and take my vision to the next level.

"Maybe one day," I promised my team of spirits.

Luckily I didn't need a life-threatening illness. They found a much more ingenious excuse. I host a regular Monday night Spirit Social where different speakers are invited to come and share their spiritual and healing modalities. I have guest speakers from all aspects of New Age and spirituality, from mediums and psychics to homeopaths and native healers. On this one particular Monday evening, the presenter was Susan Baroni, an accomplished astrologer. Susan regularly shares the upcoming astrological trends and other forecasting techniques. Tonight the topic was the "Birthday Chart" or "Solar Return Chart." She explained to us that where you are on your birthday sets up your astrological influences for the year. So where you are physically on the planet at the exact time of your birth actually affects the vibration of the year for you.

I'm intrigued. At the time I was going through some difficult trends, particularly in whatever house governs my business and legal affairs. I quickly jumped in, "Okay, my forty-sixth birthday is coming up in a couple of months. Since I live in Los Angeles, if I stay in Los Angeles on my birthday, is that good for me?" Susan types my birth data into her laptop and pulls up my solar return chart. She does a quick once-over and announces, "Oh no! You can't stay in Los Angeles on your birthday! That would be terrible. Terrible for finances, for business, for pretty much everything in your chart!"

I hate to be superstitious, but she has my attention. I ask, "If I'm supposed to go somewhere else, then where should I go?" Susan explains that she uses intuition, experience, and a lot of trial and error to test out possible places until she finds the perfect place for her client. That evening, I leave her with the task of finding me the best place to be, on the entire planet, for that magical moment to set up my perfect year.

About a week later, I get the call. "Do you want to know where you are going for your birthday?" I've told Susan she can pick anywhere in the world, but I'm really hoping it's not Iceland or somewhere extremely cold. A tropical and exotic location would be nice. I wait anxiously for her pronouncement.

"You're going to Brazil!" she tells me.

"Wow, Rio, cool!" I'm already envisioning a great party week, Carnival-style.

"No, actually Central Brazil, close to Brasilia," Susan says taking her role seriously.

"Um, Brazil. Exotic, nice, good weather" was my first thought. And then I had a sudden revelation. *"Wait a minute, I think that's where John of God is from!"*

We looked up John of God together on the Internet and sure enough, that's where he was! *"Well,"* I thought to myself smiling, *"you sneaky spirits. You found a way to get me to Brazil to see John of God with a most definite date and excuse."* What really tickled me, though, was what Susan said during her reading of my astrology chart—the one that applied if I did make the trip to that area of Brazil.

Susan declared, "I see you doing 'spiritual journeys'." Then she clarified, "I'm not sure whether it is physically taking people on journeys, or whether it's metaphysically."

I giggled to myself because she didn't know that the name I had chosen for my documentary series and workshops was "Gail Thackray's Spiritual Journeys." Yes, I was actually physically taking people on journeys, and also metaphysically, through film, media, and spiritual awareness. John of God was going to be the perfect addition to this documentary series, I thought.

The rest of Susan's reading highlighted a much rosier picture for my year, especially with the legal matters I had inquired about. Not only were the health, financial, and legal areas to be good, but there was a particular emphasis on my spiritual teachings. I would be leaving my small arena and blossoming to a worldwide audience. *"I'm ready!"* I thought. I really had no idea of what was to come!

So that is how the spirits were able to give me an excuse to go to

Brazil and get me going. I've now come to hear many other examples of the spirits gently working people towards visiting John of God, long before they ever make that trip. Of course that's often how Spirit guides us, if we would only pay attention. The Spirits from this wonderful place in Brazil seem to be particularly persistent, and my guides seem to have a purpose in my being there. I was trying my best to listen.

So I decide to go for it. I've justified this as my birthday present to myself. After all, it could save my life if my chart in Los Angeles accurately predicted a horrible year. At the very least, this should be a fun little vacation. I'll also get to check it out for my new documentary series, I reasoned. In truth, I think I had an inclination that my purpose in going was something far greater. I go ahead and book my flight. I'm going by myself. I don't know anybody down there. I don't even know where to stay or how to plan my trip, but I know I'll figure it out.

As it gets closer to the time, funnily enough, I meet people who've been there before. They offer to give me phone numbers of friends and other tips. I start to hear more and more about this amazing man, John of God, and his healing center—the "Casa." Everything just seemed to fall into place beautifully, like I was absolutely meant to go. Of course, my husband thinks I'm completely crazy!

Subconsciously, I knew I was being guided from a higher level and that this was going to be a life-changing trip. The spirits had a purpose for me. There was a reason to go on this journey and to go by myself. I didn't know what or why, but I felt that on this one, I needed to trust.

CHAPTER 3

Arriving in Brazil

I LAND IN BRAZIL just in time to check in at the hotel, have a quick lunch, and head off to the Casa for the afternoon session. It's a beautiful Brazilian afternoon. My hotel, or as they call it here, a *pousada*, is small and quaint, but pretty and with a vibration that makes you immediately feel a loving, nurturing energy. The garden patio is arranged around a central flowing waterfall feature that immediately soothes the senses. The flowers are bright, tropical, and fragrant, and there is a clean fresh smell of recent rainfall that quickly dried in the sun. The Buddhist meditation room and the natural spa décor give the impression that our spiritual rejuvenation is being taken care of here. Whether it's the beautiful Brazilian sunshine or whether there really is a supernatural healing protection zone, I don't know at this point, but there is a feeling of sublime surrender in the air.

Still not knowing a soul, I must admit I did have a fleeting thought of *"Oh my, what have I done? I don't know anyone here and does anyone even speak English?!"* Actually, this particular hotel is mostly frequented by Scandinavians and Germans. Being a typical Brit, I don't even know a few words in any other language. I look to the spirits for guidance, "Who could I talk to?" I make a beeline to a table with three German guys. Smiling cutely, I invite myself. They are particularly accommodating and happen to speak a little bit of English. I scored! I introduce myself and they are eager to be friendly and share their stories of how they happened to be in this little town in the middle of nowhere in central Brazil. My unsuspecting tour guides brief me on the Casa protocols and meeting John of God. I find out that when one of the healing spirits incorporates within him, which means the Spirit uses his body to perform healings, this is when people refer to him as "John of God" or the "Entity." When he is not incorporated, people simply call him "Medium João" (João being the name for John in Portuguese).

I am amused at this group of what looks like Harley Davidson bikers, or perhaps they were German rocker dudes. Definitely not the kind of guys I would expect to be here, meditating in this quiet place in Brazil and passionately discussing topics of spirit connection and emotional healing.

I listen intently as this one tough-looking guy, Eric, shares his personal revelations. He explains that his profound spiritual experience here was many trips previous, and this time he came for just a spiritual "tune-up." He shares that two years earlier he had terrible back pain as a result of a motorcycle accident (my assumption of Harley-riding bikers was confirmed!). Eric had received a lot of injuries, and even after multiple surgeries, he'd been told by his doctors that he would continue to be in pain.

Somebody told him about John of God and how this great sage had miraculously healed even the most difficult physical injuries. Eric made the trip. He had bravely volunteered to be one of the two or three subjects a day that receive an actual physical surgery, given on stage as a demonstration of a "miracle." John of God, incorporated with a spirit from the other side, had performed this physical surgery. This was an example of one of the most controversial surgeries that John of God performs regularly and is normally the focus of the many "debunk or real?" documentaries about him. This is what I call "The Thing-Up-the-Nose Surgery." John of God first puts his subjects under some kind of spiritual anesthesia, and then the Spirit or Entity working through Medium João actually puts a large instrument (a very scary surgical instrument, like giant forceps) up one nostril. If that's not enough, he turns the instrument about, with all the bone-crunching sound effects, and then pulls it out, sometimes with a sudden gush of blood and flesh. All the while, the person apparently feels nothing and remains completely motionless.

Eric reports the same thing: seeing the forceps going up his right nostril, feeling pressure but no pain. Then experiencing the rush of blood covering his shirt as if he were a bystander watching, rather than a person being operated on without anesthesia. He didn't feel anything, he emphasizes, still in amazement several years later. Eric describes it as an odd experience where he felt completely calm and almost detached. He didn't feel any pain, he assures me for about the tenth time. Still, I wince at the thought as the images run through my mind.

Incredibly, the next day he woke up with no back pain at all. He didn't know how "the surgery" could have done anything for his back, yet it did.

"But what was even more amazing," he exclaims, "this scar was not from my accident, this appeared after this physical surgery." Eric holds out his arm, clearly displaying a long thin scar almost the full length of his arm. "This arm was very weak after the accident, but when I woke up from the spiritual operation it was completely back to normal except for this new scar!" What I found most intriguing was that Eric believed that this surgery not only helped him physically, it somehow helped him emotionally and mentally; that his life changed drastically for the better. Now Eric comes to this remote little town about every year or so, just for a sort of tune-up, a kind of gratitude trip. To my amazement, I was to hear similar stories over and over!

It was almost surreal to be sitting with these pseudo-macho guys, each sharing the humility, the enlightenment, and the spiritual guidance they were receiving in their lives from having been connected to this energy. What struck me was that they were not trying to sell me or convince me, but rather I was doing the asking. There was no validation needed from their end. There was a feeling that they absolutely believed this and that they had complete confidence that there were spirits here capable of miracles. Clearly their lives were much more connected, not only here but back home as well. I was getting more and more excited about my journey. What miracles was I going to experience?

It is now time for the afternoon Casa session, and my new German friends invite me to join them. I'm so excited that I'm finally going to meet this super-human healer, John of God. We begin the short stroll down the dusty streets of this little rural village to the Casa. The wind-blown red dirt paths lead us past a few free-range chickens, and we receive a greeting from the odd stray but healthy-looking mutt. As we pass the other pousadas, more and more people, all dressed in white, join in. With their outfits glistening in the Brazilian sun, they look almost angel-like. We arrive at the Casa, a gated but inviting compound. I found it quite miraculous that one can actually feel a very special sacred energy, like a loving powerful energy field oozing out of the gates. It's a pretty place to look at, but when viewed with one's other senses, it is even more beautiful.

The colors of the buildings, turquoise-blue and white, remind me a little bit of a public swimming pool, but very neat and clean-looking. However, the surrounding gardens give it a more charming atmosphere. It is a little bit like a Spanish mission, situated on a plateau overlooking miles and miles of lush green valleys. The gardens have small rambling walkways, patches of vibrant tropical colors, and many wooden benches where you can sit and meditate. The whole atmosphere is very quiet and peaceful. Walking through these gardens, I got the distinct feeling that spirits were walking beside me—loving benevolent spirits, actually touching and talking to me. This was the strongest, most real spirit connection I had felt to date.

Hundreds of people are arriving, excitedly whispering about the many miracles they're experiencing. My new friends help me through the organizational protocols of the Casa, showing me, "the newbie," what to do. First I will need to see one of the Casa translators. He will write down on a piece of paper to be presented to John of God what I would like healed. They also tell me about the "first-timers' line." This is where I start, where I go in front of John of God in Entity for an energy scan to begin being guided on my spiritual journey.

Some of my friends are going inside the chapel-like rooms to start the "current." I later learn that approximately half the people at any given session choose or are guided to sit in meditation in one of the inner "current" rooms alongside many established Casa mediums. This large group meditation, working with thousands of benevolent spirits, creates the loving warm energy through which the spirits channel. This energy John of God calls "Currencia" or the "Current."

I enter the Great Hall to wait for my line to be called. The Great Hall probably fits three hundred people, and it is full and buzzing, with every chair taken and every standing space filled. This large crowd is excitedly gathered, quietly whispering, waiting for an appearance from the great healer. Some are in wheelchairs. Some have obvious physical difficulties. There is a real air of caring and courtesy from everyone as they move over to help others get a better view or assist those with wheelchairs to the front. Everyone is wearing their white outfits, which we are told helps the spirits to be able to read our energy better. Beautiful piped music plays over the speakers and sets the tone. There is a stage at the front with several speakers taking turns, talking to the crowd. Some speak in English or are accompanied by a translator. Others speak Portuguese, German, or another language. Even the ones in a foreign language are so inspirational you feel moved, even if you don't understand them. As I am sitting in this large waiting area, I feel like I have people around me that are in spirit, that are really close to me, talking to me and taking care of me.

Now, I'm used to communicating with spirits, but this seems so different. The spirits here feel so much closer, like they are sitting next to me and talking to me. I can feel the odd brush across my face, and it is hard to decipher if it is a breeze from one of the many fans placed around the hall or if it is, in fact, a brush with spirit. There is definitely a feeling of love here. But is it from the group of people waiting in this hall who periodically smile and seem to be subconsciously sending me caring and compassion? Or is it the heavenly beings that are here? Or is it perhaps some mixture of the two?

Then the moment everyone has been waiting for arrives. This great man, the phenomenon, John of God, steps out onto the stage.

CHAPTER 4

First Day at the Casa

S JOHN OF GOD enters, there is a distinct feeling of awe to have this powerful man so close and accessible. A feeling of immense love seems to emanate from his body, and every person in the room is captivated by his presence. There is barely a whisper as we each stare in wonderment that such a godly presence is in front of us. Hundreds of people crowd around the small stage, straining their heads for a better view. He addresses the crowd in his native Portuguese, slowly and softly, while several translators summarize for the rest of us. It doesn't matter if we don't understand, we're glued to every word.

Medium João looks like a sweet, very caring, but unassuming soul. The sense is that there is no ego here, just another day in his selfless devotion to the work of God. He beckons for some of his regular mediums to come close and hold his hands. He then bends over as if in pain and gasps loudly, sucking in air. One would immediately rush to his aid if this hadn't been something he had been doing twice a day for decades. As Medium João stands up straight, his eyes roll back and up to the ceiling before returning to the normal position. Something very special is happening. It is clear that this is now "John of God," a powerful healing spirit, directing

Medium João's physical human body.

Have I just witnessed a direct channeling of a spirit going into and incorporating in a human body? There is now a completely different presence on the stage. A highly advanced and enlightened being of a completely different persona is now addressing us. An energy glow appears to emanate, like a massive golden aura that seems to radiate twenty feet in all directions. *"Can anyone else see this?"* I wonder. I am certain everyone can at least sense this warm, loving energy field. John of God's eyes look glazed over, and he doesn't appear to be using them to focus on anything. I was not close enough to see today but would later confirmed that his eyes do in fact change from brown to a surreal aqua blue that would indicate the soul in occupancy is in fact from another world.

Each session one spirit incorporates into John of God. There are the main spirit workers. These twenty or more "regulars" are pretty recognizable to those at the Casa. Other spirits incorporate less often. They are all benevolent light workers. Each spirit has its own personality—after all, they were all different people in life. Sometimes a person may even be asked to come back another day when a more appropriate spirit for the person's healing will be incorporated.

Two volunteers are brought up on the stage. Both look like they are under some kind of spiritual trance. As John of God prepares his first volunteer for an eye-scraping surgery, he invites any medical doctors and film crews to come close so that they can see the operation in full detail. John of God is presented with a tray of a few "surgical" items, though there is a definite lack of sterilized gloves and protocol. Slowly, deliberately, and somewhat trance-like, John of God takes what appears to be a simple kitchen knife and begins to scrape the man's eyeball. The man does not flinch. A Swiss doctor is standing inches away, excitedly commenting on the operation. He can hardly believe what he is seeing, as it goes completely against his medical training.

After completing the first "surgery" John of God takes his next volunteer, positions him firmly against the wall, and lifts up the man's shirt, exposing his abdomen to the crowd. John of God now takes a surgical knife. This one at least appeared to be in a sterile wrapper. Then, with no anesthetic and no surgical gloves, the performing doctor in-spirit makes an incision in the man's abdomen. John of God places two fingers deep into the incision and seems to wiggle them around in the man's flesh. He completes the operation with a surgical needle and thread.

Even toward the back of the room, straining to see between people's heads, I am convinced that there is no kind of trickery involved. And seeing that they encourage anyone who wants to come close, including doctors and filmmakers, I am further assured. The volunteers are quietly laid down on a medical gurney and led off to the recovery area. Without stopping for applause or explanation, John of God slowly and deliberately turns to enter his Entity room, where he will take a seat and see hundreds of people in turn. The rest wait in the Great Hall to be called into line.

To be honest, I'm not feeling the best physically right now. I can feel a headache coming on, and I'm wondering if the long flight has caught up with me. I've been sitting in the Great Hall closing my eyes and trying to meditate, waiting for the big John of God appearance. This is the room where everybody gathers before being treated. The people here have their ailments and their issues; they've not yet been cleansed. I don't know if I am picking up on those vibes or whether the energy is just too strong, but at this point I have a really bad headache that won't subside. Then this voice comes to me, just like a person standing next to me.

"Well, go lie on the crystal bed" the voice suggests in response to my pleas to remove my headache.

Unsure of how to do this but willing to follow orders from this invisible guide, I leave the hall in search of the crystal beds. I'm told that you have to schedule an appointment at the bookstore, but they fill up quickly and I probably can't get one for today. I go off to inquire anyway, hoping I'll get lucky. As it so happens, I am told that there is one space available, right now.

"I did get lucky," I thought, or was it Divine Intervention?

The crystal bed looks like a regular twin bed but it has a metal framework that holds seven quartz crystals that hang from above and run partway down the length of the bed. These seven perfectly shaped clear quartz crystals are aligned so that they point toward each *chakra* (energy center) on the body. A colored light shines through each crystal to the client. The color corresponds to the color of the chakra that it points to. The attendant adjusts the crystals slightly so that each is aligned and pointing to my different chakras. I pondered for a moment. In Reiki I had learned about chakras but had presumed this was an Eastern philosophy. I was surprised to find that in this little remote village, chakras seemed to be accepted by everyone and they happened to be exactly the same as those in my Reiki teachings. Still, I thought this all seemed a little far-fetched. I'm going to somehow feel a colored light, pointing at me? I doubted I'd feel anything. I was about to be very surprised!

As I lay there, I felt relaxed and soothed, listening to the gentle music playing. Then almost immediately, I experienced a floating out-of-body feeling that I have sometimes felt during very deep meditation. I started to have visions and messages. It was a beautiful, serene feeling as I drifted in and out of colorful soothing visuals. I felt like the spirits were in the room, touching my head gently and talking to me. The spirits were so close that I actually felt their fingers gently massaging my forehead and my headache gradually disappearing. I could feel fingertips working on my temples just as if a real therapist were in the room and lightly touching my head. It was so real that after my session was over and the attendant came to remove the cover from my eyes, I didn't stir immediately. I thought it was still the spirits! The spirits' work was definitely clearing my headache, and by the time the twenty minutes were up, it had almost completely gone.

Toward the end of my session, a tropical rainstorm decided to pass through, adding to the surreal protected feeling I was experiencing. I'm lying on the crystal bed when the sound of the rain comes—first in single intermittent drops, then rapidly progressing to a tropical downpour. Drops hit the top of the tin roof, pitter-patter. I reveled in the beauty of this tropical storm moving through, cleansing and revitalizing everything she touches.

Feeling better, I can now return to the Great Hall. However, because of the heavy rain, I find myself taking shelter. I sit waiting on the benches beneath the awning, quietly enjoying the rhythmic raps on the tin roof. I guess the spirits didn't think it was my time in line yet. The message came from spirit that I was to sit down a little while: "Just sit and enjoy this cleansing." Within a few minutes, the sky cleared and the sun peeked out. The birds are chirping as I stroll through the newly watered gardens, back up to the Great Hall again. Now my headache is completely gone. I feel completely cleansed and revitalized, and I know this was all orchestrated by Spirit.

As soon as I get near the Great Hall, I start to feel my head becoming cloudy and dense again. The spirits intervene: "No, just keep waiting outside" is the message. So for a while, I rotate from meditating on the benches to taking a stroll in the gardens. Worried about missing my place in line, I keep doing the rounds, double-checking on which lines have been called.

Again the message from Spirit is, "No, just wait outside."

As I'm sitting in the garden meditating and admiring the view, I suddenly get the message, "Go eat."

I respond, "But I'm not hungry." And they say, "No, go eat."

"But I'm not hungry," I protest.

"Just go eat!"

I do as I'm told and walk over to the little Casa cafe. I see some of my German friends. As I approach, Eric asks me if my line has been called. I confidently tell him that I've got plenty of time until my line is due up. Eric takes it upon himself to double-check on my behalf. He comes running back in a panic, telling me that the first-timers are almost done and I'm going to miss my place in line! At that, several Casa volunteers rush me through the halls and right up to the front of the line, skipping the hall wait entirely and placing me next in line to see John of God. I pondered how the spirits arranged everything to have me go to the cafe just in time to see Eric, who in turn decided to check in for me. All this so that the spirits could get me to the front of the line without having any more problems with the energy.

CHAPTER 5

In Front of John of God

I NOW FIND MYSELF about to be face to face with the great spirit that is incorporated in John of God. It is an awe-inspiring moment such as one would expect if they were about to have physical contact with a saint. A moment in time that will be carved blissfully into my memory. I'm slightly nervous but in complete awe.

I've been rushed through the Great Hall and into the sacred inner chapel, where John of God is seated. This powerful being is holding court from a large, throne-like chair, adding to the grandeur of my experience. A huge rose quartz crystal adorned with rosaries and other catholic icons separates John of God's throne from the rest. There is one more first-timer before me. I scan the room. Probably a hundred people are seated in church-like pews. All are deep in meditation, their eyes closed, deep in thought or trance. Some are sitting quietly while others are making facial expressions and hand movements as they communicate with invisible spirits. All are in a world of their own. Closer to John of God, the meditators are seated in more comfortable chairs. These are the Casa mediums, the established energy channelers.

I had heard of these mediums back in Los Angeles, and part of me was thinking that my purpose here was to be chosen by John of

God as a medium. I had fantasies that I would be recognized by him and called forward for my talent to heal people. After all, I could communicate with spirits and I was a Reiki Master and healer. Perhaps my purpose here was to take my healing to another level and to heal those in need here. I was soon put in my place.

"Leave your ego at the door!" I was told by Spirit. "You are here for healing, too."

I am now standing in the aura of this great and powerful being while possessing the ego of a wallflower. *"Something so much greater than I, than all of us together,"* I thought. *"Something completely overwhelming, completely humbling, yet completely loving, is working here."* I feel honored to have this experience.

I notice that next to John of God is one special medium's chair. I am surprised to see Michael, one of my new German friends, seated there. Michael had very modestly mentioned that he felt close to Medium João and that he had been chosen by him as a medium, even though he felt undeserving of this honor. I had clearly chosen well in adopting my human guides. I jokingly called him Angel Michael from then on.

As I wait my turn, I am absorbing the most loving beautiful energy that surrounds this room. It feels warm and cozy. In fact, I ponder if the whole room actually has a different color hue than the outer rooms. Is this a natural effect of the sunlight coming through the blinds? It certainly has a golden angelic glow. I feel loving spirits touching me and holding me as I stand there, gently caressing my face and stroking my hair. It almost feels like angel wings surrounding me. I am now standing about five feet in front of

John of God, waiting my turn. I am sure I am within his luminous aura. Standing here feels like I am standing in the presence of God himself.

I am clutching, in anticipation, the note that the Casa translator wrote for me in Portuguese, the note that will be presented to John of God. I had told my translator, "Well, I have some fibroids in my uterus and a few other physical things here and there that I would like to fix. But my attention is most on spiritual enlightenment, that's what I really want." *But wouldn't the spirits know why I'm here?* I mused to myself. The translator scribbled something brief on the piece of paper. I was to learn later that, yes, the spirits do know our requests; however, we must always ask for our healing. It is not up to the spirits to decide if we would like to heal a certain area of our life, as then they would be taking on our karma. Once again, an example that we can receive all that we desire in our life, if we only ask!

Now is the big moment. This all-powerful being using the body of Medium João turns his attention to me. The Entity has already begun my diagnosis. He is holding my hand and gazing through me, reading my energy field. He doesn't appear to take any notice as the translator whispers the words from my paper. I am frozen in awe, like I am being held by an angelic energy. My heart is jittery but still I feel a sense of stillness. I feel the loving caress from this beautiful being—pure unconditional love. The whole experience takes maybe five seconds, but it seems like a moment held in eternity. The Spirit in Entity quickly diagnoses, "Surgery!" I smile in heartfelt gratitude as I am directed off in a daze.

I am to come back tomorrow for the morning session, first up with the group of people receiving surgeries. It seems a little drastic since I don't have a life-threatening illness like so many others who come here, but I am honored. It's a good start to my trip. Now I have a choice: I can either have a physical surgery such as the volunteers I saw on stage earlier today, or I can have an invisible surgery.

It didn't take much debate. I'm thinking, *"Heck no! There is no way I am going to go for a physical surgery!"* With my luck I'd get "The Thing-Up-the-Nose Surgery" that Eric had. I don't think I could deal with that one and got queasy at the thought. Luckily, it is your choice; no one is told to get a physical surgery. Everybody gets an invisible surgery unless you volunteer and say that you would like a physical surgery. It was also explained that physical surgeries are no stronger than invisible ones, they are just to help people to believe in what is happening.

"I believe, I believe!" I told myself.

My first day at the Casa has been quite eventful. My German guides and a few others gathered at the Casa café excitedly reciting the day's events. Michael and the others who had been in the meditation current impressed me with their excitement about various healings that had taken place on people they didn't even know. They were thrilled that this person was starting to regain strength and another person's cancerous tumor was reducing in size. How nice, I thought, to watch these people honestly caring more about others than for themselves—an admirable trait I was to see often at the Casa. Perhaps this wasn't so unusual for me to see in women, but I couldn't help compare these men with my not-socompassionate-and-caring relationship back home.... Was I being asked to take notice by Spirit, or was this just a deep feminine need surfacing?

Off we go for a quick regroup at Frutti's juice bar, the central point of the sum-total night life in this sleepy town: a couple of juice bars and a few very small restaurants. Sipping a smoothie made from fresh acaí berry, I decided this must be the most delicious healthy drink I'd ever had.

I took out my camera and we snapped a few shots of each other, friends on vacation. When we looked on the camera screen, we were stunned at what we saw.

"Wow! Look at that!"

"That's crazy!"

The most amazing was a picture of me and two of the guys with what looked like streaks of energy coming out of my Crown Chakra, bouncing all over the table, and connecting back to my friends. We took multiple pictures, and this energy appeared to be coming right off the top of my head in several of them. Was this some kind of weird camera error? Or is this really the energy that one receives after going in front of John of God? Has my Crown Chakra been blown wide open and is this why I felt like my head was about to explode in the waiting room? Had I been blessed to receive just a small remnant of the powerful energy I had felt in the presence of John of God? We would take many more pictures on that trip. My camera seemed to have a mind of its own, deciding when it would flash and snap. The resulting pictures were unlike any I've ever taken before or since.

As we watch the sun setting over the vast Brazilian landscape, its beauty reminds me of that famous spiritual quotation I must have heard somewhere (or perhaps it was whispered from the other side): "God can be seen in everything, if you only open your eyes."

Very soon it is morning. Time for my spiritual surgery! The Casa volunteers usher all those having a surgery into a small inviting room with pews, a little like a chapel, with paintings of saints and catholic icons. However, here there are also paintings of the spirits who work at the Casa. A calming, sweet Brazilian lady instructs us to close our eyes and to relax and meditate. I'm nervous, but I don't know why because nothing is going to physically happen to me. I try to calm myself. *"I am not doing the physical surgery, nobody is going to cut me up or do anything,"* I continually reassure myself. I don't understand why I'm so nervous, but I am. The beautiful Brazilian guide is speaking softly and calmly, praising God and the spirits and talking us through a little meditation in a mixture of Portuguese and English. Gently, I feel the soft touch of spirits and a warm current of loving energy.

My eyes are tightly closed but I am dying to take a peek. I physically feel the spirits stroking my face, lightly pressing on my shoulders, and just kind of calming me, telling me that I'll be okay. They are very close now and they feel almost as real as the people sitting on either side of me. There are several spirits around, not just one but a whole team. I couldn't open my eyes even if I'd wanted to. I feel like I've been hypnotized into creating heavy eyelids that refused to open. Then with our eyes still closed, there is a sudden shift of energy in the room as if a major draft blew through, but it was not a temperature change. We feel the presence of John of God in Entity come in the room. It's as if a golden aura of love precedes this beautiful being. John of God says a few words in Portuguese that resemble a prayer. There is an enlightened feeling of love throughout the room. Then the translator says to us that if we want to have a *physical* surgery to raise our hand, but to keep our eyes closed. My hand is glued to my knee. There is no way I'm putting my hand up! I'm nervous enough about having an invisible surgery.

John of God continues his prayers. His voice has the melody of a thousand angels, soothing, comforting, and healing. I know there are many special energies in the room now. Medium or no medium, everyone has to be feeling this change, I am convinced. I ask nervously, "Who is here, who is doing my surgery, who is working on me?" The face of Jesus slowly materializes in a kaleidoscope of colors, close to my face, just to my left, smiling and loving. The vision is strong and clear and the energy that accompanies this vision is heavenly, calming, and beautiful. Now, I'm not religious and Jesus is not somebody that I would normally have thought about, which makes it all the more believable to me. I feel very honored and eternally grateful.

The energy is broken with the translator's announcement: "You can now open your eyes. Your surgery is complete." I open my eyes and look around the room. The whole process felt like maybe five or ten minutes, so I am utterly amazed at what I see. I don't know what happened to time because as I scan the room, there are all these people that have had physical surgeries laid out on stretchers around the room. *"How could this be?"* I wonder. I didn't hear anything and this wasn't possible in the little time that passed. Yet there were six or seven people lying on gurneys who look like they had been wheeled directly from an operating room. I felt overwhelmed at the incredible power of this beautiful soul, John of God. *"Did this person, this man, have a direct connection to God?"* I thought.

I stand to leave, a little in awe of what had just taken place in those few minutes. Did I just completely lose time? I stumble out of the room into the warm Brazilian sunshine feeling like I'm floating, not quite walking. Feeling great but a little spacey.

We are instructed to write down our name and the pousada where we are staying so that the spirits could continue to work on us in our hotel room and, on the seventh night from now, remove any psychic stitches. *"Strange,"* I thought. *"Surely these miraculous beings would know where to find me,"* but dizzily I write down my details.

We are informed that the spirits would continue to work on us for the next seven days. For the next twenty-four hours we are instructed to remain in our room and not to come out. Not for food, not for anything. We are not to talk to anybody, not be on our computer, not even read a book. Just to lie as quietly as possible, meditate and sleep. Wow! Am I going to go stir crazy? I'm thinking some of this doesn't apply to me as I'm here by myself and who's going to feed me?

Even with these instructions, some people think maybe they don't really need to stay in their room for the full twenty-four hours and they'll just go back to the Casa and enjoy the energy.

We are told in no uncertain terms not to come back to the Casa for at least twenty-four hours. After spiritual surgery, your Crown Chakra is blown wide open and it may be difficult to tolerate the strong energy at the Casa, and it could give you a headache.

Other instructions are no spicy food, no pepper, no pork, no alcohol, and no sex for forty days!!! Whoops, rewind, had I heard this correctly? Perhaps I should have checked the fine print beforehand. There is a lot of talk at our pousada about if everyone could go without any pepper for forty days! (joking!). I asked one of the volunteers if sex by yourself counted, and he rolled his eyes with the unfortunate message as to the extent of my celibacy. Something to do with your energy and how stimulating energy in your body could offset the energy work of the spirits. Okay, I could understand, I suppose, and would try my best to comply. My husband might not be quite as understanding. I pondered why no spicy food, and if spicy food and sex had the same level of energy stimulation for some people!

If the post-surgery instructions seemed rather strange, the whole process was about to get a whole lot stranger.

CHAPTER 6

First Surgery

I AM BACK in my hotel room about to hunker down for the next twenty-four hours. I'm committed to be as quiet and as meditative as possible, but I'm worried that I'm going to go stir crazy. *"Just relax,"* I kept reassuring myself, *"We're in for the long haul."* I feel very protected and surreal lying in my bed, listening to the sounds of nothingness, except the odd bird chirping. *"This is going to be quite a nice experience,"* I try to convince myself.

After only a few minutes of lying in bed, I suddenly feel the spirits working on me. This is a new sensation, like somebody is touching my temples. It feels like someone is positioning me, positioning my head as if to get ready. They are touching both sides of my temples, almost like real fingers but not quite. It reminds me of when my teenage daughter got one of those abdominal toning belts, where the little electric current squeezes your tummy muscles. You feel like you are actually contracting your muscles and you are, but it's really the electricity that's doing it. It was kind of similar to that sensation—like I could really feel somebody touching my temples, but I knew somehow it was more like electricity. This was a very distinct sensation, very clear and definite. It wasn't a continuous feeling. It was more like the spirits would come in and give me this signal to mean "We are working on you." At the same time, I'd feel a "woo-woo" sensation, like *"Whoa, I need to lie down right now."* This was something I had never experienced before. This was to become my special signal from Spirit to get ready to be worked on!

Over the next few hours, as I lay there quietly, I would feel spiritual presences come into my room. I would feel the "signal" and I'd be worked on for a few minutes. Then they would leave without fanfare. It was as if they weren't present the whole time. I would get my temple sensation to let me know, "Okay, get ready, we need you to concentrate and relax now." Then I would sense the spirits coming in.

As the spirits came into my room to work on me, of course I'm asking, "Okay, who's here? Who is this? What are you doing on me? What do you look like?" and other things a medium might normally ask. It was a nice comfortable feeling that I was being taken care of by the spirits. It was not scary at all, but still a small part of me was a little nervous about this otherworldly attention.

After a team of spirits positions me and comforts me, the first "Spirit Healer" comes. He appears to be busily working on my abdomen. I ask who is he and if I can "see him" and sense his energy. He tells me his name is Dr. Klaus. He's very matter of fact and he is working on my fibroids. (Fibroids are like small round benign tumors in the womb.) I envision this person in spirit, working on my body, actually removing these dense energy balls. "What are you doing?" I ask.

"I just do the physical part; I'm only here to remove these. I don't do any of the spiritual side of it, that's for somebody else," he responds. I do see him in my mind's eye removing fleshy masses, as if I am really in a surgery. I can see him quite clearly, a very tall, very slim doctor, almost too thin and lanky. He is wearing a suit—very modern-looking. He wears glasses and has his hair cut shorter at the back and a little longer on the top.

A few days later, I asked the German group if there is such a doctor known to work at the Casa, as I didn't see a painting of him on the wall, nor had I heard his name. Many of the spirits are regular workers at the Casa and so have been "seen" and experienced by many of the mediums. When I describe his looks in more detail, he is instantly recognized. "Oh, yes, he's a doctor that lives in Germany. He wrote a book about the work of John of God and he visits often."

"You mean he's alive?" I asked.

"Yes," they replied.

"Um … gets stranger by the minute," I thought to myself.

The next spirit that comes to work on me has an overwhelmingly beautiful energy. As his presence enters my room, I feel such compassion and love. I am being cradled in a beautiful cocoon. This wonderful, loving man is kneeling at the side of my bed, and his gentle energy is healing me. I say to him, "Hmm, you look, kind of like, Dom Inácio." (St. Ignatius of Loyola, also know as Dom Inácio, founded the Society of Jesus (Jesuits) and is for whom the healing center of John of God is named; the "Casa de Dom Inácio.") "You look a little like him, like the pictures that are hanging in the Casa, but not quite the same." The man that I am looking at now, in my room, is almost completely bald and he has a very fluffy beard. Yet in the Casa paintings, Dom Inácio has a close-trimmed beard and at least some hair. Dom Inácio smiles at me and explains, "When they paint your picture, they always try to be complimentary and make you look younger, but this is the real me." What a beautiful sweet energy!

Many beautiful energies came and worked on me. Sometimes I inquired, other times I just allowed myself to relax and concentrate on the visions and messages they were giving me. It seemed more important for me to use my energy to see my life lessons and not to be so concerned with who was assisting me. I was grateful to each beautiful soul that helped me. Somehow, I knew that their genuine service was benefiting their growth in the spirit world as well. Their unconditional love and their dedication to healing were raising their vibration in the afterlife. When the spirit "doctors" were not working on me, there were still many, many other spirits watching over me. There was one that was my continual companion, a simple Jesuit priest who faithfully sat by my bedside in charge of my care and comfort for this period of time.

After perhaps an hour or two of lying in bed and being worked on periodically by Spirit, I sat up for a moment to take a sip of my blessed water. As I sat up, I felt something wet in my right nostril and instinctively put my hand up to my face. As I looked down I became slightly concerned because there was blood on my fingers. Curious, I leaned over to the mirror. Sure enough, blood was running down my right nostril! I am not one who gets nosebleeds; I hadn't knocked it or done anything to cause one, yet here it was, clearly a nosebleed without any apparent cause or pain and only on the right side. Nervously, I laughed to the spirits, "Guess I was getting 'The Thing-Up-the-Nose Surgery' after all!"

The hours passed in my room, but I was far from bored, far from being alone. Some spirits would stay for a while, others would come and go. I'm used to communicating with spirits, but this was deeper, clearer, a more intense experience—profound healing, profound understanding, an ultimate feeling of love and peace.

It became quite apparent that the spirits were working on my chakras in turn. Each energy center is an invisible swirling energy field in our body; each one resembles a cone of colorful energy, rotating like a vortex. The spirits were spending time on each energy center, clearing and bringing up any unresolved issues in those areas, before moving on to the next chakra. This wasn't anything that had been mentioned by anyone else at the Casa, but it was quite obviously true. The gap between spiritual healing modalities was once again closing. This spiritual energy felt comfortable and familiar. Of course, it should; was this not the same spiritual energy that I had been working with back home? Was spiritual healing energy and working with spirits the same anywhere in the world, no matter what your religious beliefs?

It was then revealed to me: the source of the healing energy that felt so wonderful was in fact Divine Source, or God as one may call it. These beautiful healing spirits modestly declared that they were not the source of this energy but rather were simply directing and working with this energy. After all, are we not all spiritual energies, each working to improve our soul? Whether here in the physical or in the invisible realms, are we not trying to better ourselves and to raise our vibration through helping others? Are we not one and the same, all part of Divine energy? The real source of this beautiful feeling was God.

The spirits started at my Base Chakra, the energy center at the tailbone that emanates down toward the ground. They then progressed up my body, in order of the seven main chakras, throughout the next twenty-four hours, working all the way up to my Crown Chakra.

Different spirits seemed to work on the different chakras. Some areas took more time than others. The first or Base Chakra seemed to take an hour or two; the second chakra that governs relationships and money took, oh, like most of the day!

From Reiki I understood that the Base Chakra is the chakra that is about your family, your base support, your early childhood, your life purpose, and how you see yourself in the world. As the spirits worked in this area, it reminded me of my dad, who passed away when I was seven years old. I reminisced fondly about some of my early childhood memories. I re-lived the deep pain and abandonment I felt through losing him, and I re-experienced many wonderful, touching moments that I had long since forgotten. Each memory came to me as real and as emotionally powerful as the day it happened. I laughed and I cried. I was shown specific memories that had an emotional impact on me, as opposed to what an outsider might recall as important events. Afterwards I felt refreshed and released, like my unresolved childhood anguish had left and only fond memories remained.

Then we moved to my Sacral Chakra, just below the belly button, which is the area where my fibroids were. This is the relationship area and, boy, did that area need some work! I started reminiscing about different relationships that I had experienced and, in each, delving deep into the feelings that had made an impression on me. Feelings of stabbing heartache, vulnerability, and betrayal, as well as intense passion and happiness were replayed for consideration, process, and release. There wasn't a particular order of events or a timeline, but more like different feelings that impacted my life grouped together for review. Some things surprised me, like I hadn't thought about them in years. Though now when I consider these events, they were heart-wrenching, painfully crushing moments that I thought were long since forgotten. First I sobbed uncontrollably, going over and over the event, almost punishing myself. Then I went through each event with a kind of revelation. I felt like I was being shown the purpose, reliving the deep emotions, and then releasing it with love—not feeling any resentment or anger, but just the purpose of why I went through that. Now I could look back without any emotional attachment. I could even relay understanding and forgiveness to some guy who had ripped out my heart and left me in the gutter. (Perhaps feeling loving energy towards him was too much to ask.)

Often the same lessons seemed to have been presented several times with completely different relationships and in different situations. I was finally seeing these lessons, relating them together, and then releasing them. Some small moments were brought to recall. They were just fleeting moments in time, yet they held great significance and deep emotion. Had I just gone through years of therapy in a few hours? Feelings of love, passion, sexuality, resentment, and fear all surfaced with vivid, intense emotion, and all were addressed and released. I felt myself purging anger and deep, gut-wrenching sadness, and even though I cried and cried with passion, I still felt somewhat removed.

I was being asked to look at my current relationship with my husband. I knew changes needed to be made. There was also a knowing that my fibroids were energy blocks that had been formed over the years. I knew that for these physical lumps to be completely gone, I would need to resolve this area energetically, and this would again require difficult and perhaps uncomfortable changes in my life.

We moved on to my Solar Plexus Chakra and then the Heart Chakra. One of the other minor ailments I had included in my thoughts when presenting to John of God was my irregular heartbeats. They had been better since I had curbed my massive diet soda intake. But still, occasionally my heart would skip a couple of beats and then pick up again. Medical diagnosis had given it the label of "prolapsed mitral valve." It wasn't life-threatening, I had been told, but still, it was very unnerving. The spirits took a stop at my Heart Chakra and I was shown that sometimes the relationship issues had hit a heart cord and left a little psychic scar in there.

The spirits moved on to my Throat Chakra, Third Eye Chakra, and Crown Chakra, continuing to move up my body through each of the seven main energy centers, releasing and resolving issues. I also felt work being done on my eighth chakra. The eighth chakra lies above your crown and is the energy center that is for connection to the other side and develops as your psychic abilities appear.

This whole experience was the most intense for the first twenty-four hours that I was in my hotel room, but it actually continued the entire time I was in Brazil. For example, I would be sitting at dinner and I would suddenly get my familiar cue. From out of nowhere, I would feel somebody touching my temples. I'd realize, *"Oh, it's time to go lie down now"* and I'd suddenly become drowsy. That became my signal for "Now you're being worked on." Over time it became less strong and less frequent, but even when I was back home in the States, I would once in a while feel it, that sensation of, "Okay, we are here now and we are working on you." Even now, if I lie down and ask for spiritual help, I can still feel them come to me, recognized by their touch on my temples.

The spirits seemed to be around and communicating with me constantly, but for the actual spiritual healing I was receiving, they would come and work on me only as needed. While they were working on me, I felt that it was important that I be quiet and still. Having the spirits working on me wasn't all that different from a Reiki session or some of the other healing modalities I have experienced. After all, I thought, I have often said, *"It is all the same thing."* It doesn't matter whether it is Reiki, Theta Healing, shamanism, or simply prayer; it is truly God that is doing the healing. What was perhaps different was the intensity of the healing and the absolute certainty that it was taking place.

Although I was quite happy to be having such private time with Spirit, I wasn't going to pass up my hotel's wonderful buffet meals. I was prepared to sneak out and then retreat back to my room with a to-go plate. To my great surprise and without my asking, my German friends took turns bringing me meals. I never once had to come out of my hotel room. Here were these big strapping guys, one by one coming to bring me yummy plates, ask me what I wanted, and check in on me. Again, I wondered if was I being shown these masculine men that were caring and loving for a reason?

Later it became clear to me, on a spiritual level, that for one to receive love and healing, it is important to love and help one another. For in serving and genuinely giving to another, one opens up their own connection to God, allowing this beautiful energy to travel through them. This was something I would explore in depth later. Somehow this concept was being nurtured here naturally and subconsciously, in this little town. This community was thriving on this loving, caring, wonderful energy—everybody helping everybody else, and everybody wanting the opportunity to help somebody. I wondered if this was something that would stay with people or would they change once they were back home and became involved in their own busy lives? Helping those who had surgery was seen as an opportunity for people to help, to serve, and to provide for another. I was enjoying this wonderful, loving, shared purpose and genuine feeling of connection with complete strangers and being in an environment where everybody really cares about everybody else. Perhaps this is the real healing taking place here. Once again, I was being asked to look at my own life back home.

Michael brought my breakfast the next day while I was in my last few hours of retreat. I had been opened emotionally, having bared my soul to the spirits all through the night, delving into each and every relationship. I was ready to talk, and Michael sweetly listened. In fact, he too had many similar experiences, and we sat for hours relating not only our experiences, but our feelings and processing through those feelings. Normally it would have been odd to share intimate details with someone I barely knew, but I felt like I knew Michael on a soul level. It was a very comfortable and lovely morning for both of us. Perhaps the spirits had sent a physical person to talk with me as part of my spiritual treatment.

So did my physical issues resolve from this spiritual surgery? Good question. My symptoms from the fibroids and a prolapsed mitral valve seemed to almost disappear instantly. However, the moment I stepped on the plane to return to Los Angeles, the symptoms returned in full force. I had been told by the spirits that changes needed to be made in my current life to completely resolve these issues. They were correct. I had more work to do, and Spirit was definitely showing me the way. Eventually I did make those changes and it took time, but now a year later my symptoms are completely gone. I presume the physical causes of my symptoms have been removed as well, although I have not tested to verify this. What seemed more important, though, was the spiritual adjustment the surgery made in my life. Looking back, I would say the physical side was definitely secondary.

One would think that standing in front of John of God in Entity and receiving direction from the great spirit sage would be the time when your great healing and enlightenment would take place. One would expect an instantaneous healing or a wise answer right there and then. Somehow things work differently here. The spirits may work in an odd and unpredictable way, but the spirits have a perfect plan. They had a perfect plan for me that was about to unfold, as I was to learn the following week. But first, I was to get to know my new friends and even the spirits here a bit better.

CHAPTER 7

Making Friends

AFTER THE INCREDIBLE EXPERIENCE of my surgery and in-room healing, I decided to be social and venture out. I was invited by girlfriends to experience the sacred waterfall a short hike from the main grounds of the Casa. It is a very high-vibrational healing place, and one needs to ask the spirits for permission to go. I checked in with the Entities and was given the spiritual ok to visit. There are very few pictures of this waterfall, as you are asked to not take photographs. Just as Native Americans believe, if you are taking photographs, you are taking away the energy from the spirits. One would not want to remove any of the beautiful energy of this place.

As we hiked down to this blessed waterfall hidden in a glen of jungle between two majestic mountains, I fell in love. This breathtaking sacred space is where one can receive a cleansing from spirit, both inside and out. It isn't a boasting grandiose waterfall such as the Brazilian falls you see in travel brochures, but it's plentiful for one individual to stand under its cascade and feel the refreshing energy. More importantly, you feel the supernatural energies of the spirits surrounding you like a cleansing bath. I felt a whole multitude of spirits removing and dissolving any remaining negativity from my energy field, like a private spa rejuvenation.

On the way back from this spiritual cleansing, we met the Brazilian Adonis, Fabio. And yes, that was his real name! After changing his wet shirt and exposing drops of water shimmering off his perfectly sun-tanned muscular body, Fabio offered to walk me back to my hotel. How could I resist?! We strolled through town on this blissful warm Brazilian day, stopping to sip leisurely on a fruity drink and do a little gift shopping. We got to know each other as we chatted. Fabio turned out to be an attorney. Brains as well as beauty!

Then later, while we are hanging out back at my hotel, I find that this absolutely gorgeous guy can't stop looking into my eyes. Is he flirting with me? I'm quite enjoying the attention that I'm getting—strangely, something I hadn't even noticed I had been missing. So we're sipping on a glass of... blessed water (yeah, no wine here) when Eric and Ivan arrive back at the hotel and put an immediate stop to the fun.

"Hey, you know she had a spiritual surgery!" This was code for no sex for forty days. I'm like, "Hey guys–buzz kill!" I'm just kidding; I'm married. Still, the attention was nice. Yet I appreciate that my German surrogate brothers are watching over me and making sure I don't lose myself.

I have now made some wonderful friends on this trip and have come to know them pretty intimately. Our nightly communal dinner is a great way to catch up on our personal events at the Casa and to share our insights from our long sessions in meditation. We find ourselves revealing our deep hopes and dreams, our life purpose, and the true meaning of existence. We share our personal talents, including mine as a medium. I give my new friends a little sampling of messages from their loved ones in spirit. I find out that I am not allowed to do energy work on anyone, as it may interfere with the healing program the spirits have for that individual. However, bringing in people's loved ones didn't appear to break any energy rules. Messages from relatives not only shocked and surprised my friends, but they were moved and were able to release suppressed feelings. I was able to give insights from my guides, and perhaps even the spirits from the Casa were the ones delivering messages via me as the physical contact. I was happy I could help guide my new friends in this way.

We've become a very close-knit group in such a short amount of time. I find myself becoming drawn into my new friends' personal stories and spending time in the current rooms asking for favors for everyone else but me. I am hopeful that Jerry may one day walk again, and I am excited to see his progress on the bars. I am truly anguished over Penny's setback after her stage-four cancer seemed to be retreating so well. I think lovingly of my group back home, spending specific time in current on each person's ailment and making sure that everyone is receiving my thoughts and prayers. Most of all, I ask for joy and prosperity for all of my spiritual group back home.

All these wonderful experiences with my new friends and the selfless, caring way that we are all interacting got me to thinking about this very real feeling of love bringing everyone together. We genuinely care about one another. I began to wonder if this ability to love others, to care for others, and to help those whose needs are greater than one's own is somehow the key to one's own healing. There seems to be a connection. It made sense that in this spiritual healing place, people would reach out in a loving manner to a total stranger. What really struck me was the loving, caring side that is exhibited here by such masculine men. Am I being shown that this is a quality I deserve in a mate, and am I meant to see the stark difference between this and what I am receiving at home? I start to think about my world back home and long for this loving feeling to continue there.

The people who come here are from all walks of life and have many different reasons for wanting to come. What surprises me is that, yes, there are many people here with disastrous illnesses, physical impairments, but there are just as many people that come for spiritual enlightenment. The mental, emotional enlightenment is something that is received by all. Many of the people that were healed physically from a cancer or a terrible illness often come back to this place again and again, returning for more of a spiritual healing. It becomes obvious that those who had been connected to this Source energy had been changed forever.

I had been told by the spirits many times before that when they work on you and they heal, they heal at a soul level. They heal the energy around our aura and remove negative attachments or negative influences from our field. Energies of people that have not passed to the light or lower-level spirits can actually be attached to us! The healing spirits at the Casa are going to the source of the issue, and not only do they heal the physical ailments, they heal all the outer bodies as well. They cleanse and enlighten the energy field around us so that everything in our life looks better. When the spirits are able to remove this negative junk we have attracted around us, we not only have physical health, we can experience financial abundance, happiness, prosperity, and a completely different outlook on life.

Some people decide that life actually looks and feels so much better around the Casa that they stay for a long while, maybe permanently. Of course, the environment is beautiful: a picturesque sleepy town that consists of small shops and cafes, a few local farms, chickens running between banana trees, and lush vegetation. There is also a view of the valley that reminds you of heaven. One can understand why people visit the Casa and end up settling down to a new life. But it's not just the view and the lifestyle, it's a kind of feeling, an energy of a loving community. People often decide to move in for a few weeks. Sometimes that stretches to a few months, or even a few years. They become part of the Casa community, perhaps one of the Casa mediums or working as a guide for others. Some may have independent finances and just stay and play.

Sean, known as "Spikey," was one such Casa medium and guide who had come here for emotional healing and found his real purpose in life at the Casa. I had met him a few times socially and he was great fun to hang out with, but when I brought through his loved ones in spirit one evening, he sat and cried as he finally released years of heartache. This was when we truly connected and became real friends.

Kim was another who had fallen in love with the place. She

had rented a small Spanish-style villa with a girlfriend for three months and intended to experience the Casa for an extended time. I was invited to her holiday home, a little off the "strip," for dinner. Spikey and I contributed by buying the fresh vegetables and chicken, and we prepared a beautiful dinner together. While we waited for our feast to cook, we took a stroll around the neighborhood and appreciated the beautiful scenery and the quiet life. So this was daily life in Abadiânia.

On my second trip to the Casa, I took my friend Collette on a hike in the hills above the Casa to appreciate the beautiful scenery I had come to love. We snapped some shots, standing on a hill meditating with a 360-degree view of the sky as our backdrop. Beneath we could view miles and miles of unspoiled, lush green valleys. It was a beautiful warm day's hike. We had to return a little earlier than planned, though. My friend, whom I was also caring for after a recent "invisible" surgery said that she could suddenly feel tenderness and soreness in her abdomen, like you would if you'd had a "regular" surgery (which she'd had actually had in the past). We're told that even when you have an "invisible" surgery, there actually are spiritual stitches inside of you, so you have to take it easy! She wanted to go back to our pousada and rest. Perhaps I had overdone it in my zest to be a good host!

John of God is in session at the Casa on Wednesdays, Thursdays, and Fridays. But the experience is hardly closed the remainder of the week. Saturday through Tuesday, the spirits continue to guide and do their work. This is the time when people get together and get to know each other. Tuesday is a great day for community and to contribute by helping with the peeling and chopping of vegetables for the week's blessed soup. The Casa kitchen is happy to have volunteers, and it's fun to be a part of this ritual. Not only do the Casa visitors receive the soup, but plenty is made to distribute through other soup kitchens that Medium João has set up across town, where it is gratefully received by those that need it the most.

A Catholic Rosary service is held at the Casa on Friday evenings and this is popular for all, Catholic or not. Although Medium João is not normally presiding, the spirit energy clearly is. Often people report the smell of roses. I wonder if it's the same rose energy that I smelled with the icon of Mary. A regular church service is held on Sunday mornings, though this is anything but "regular." Hymns are often replaced with popular Beatles songs and John Lennon's words of love. In fact, an Entity that has come through John of God a handful of times wouldn't reveal his name. He said, "If I reveal my name, there'll be too many people coming here." So he said, "Just call me Love." People wondered, "Could it be Jesus?" but then any church will say that Jesus is there. So who could it be? Many think it is John Lennon himself. It's certainly possible, and it's a place where celebrity spirits would surely love to visit.

I had become closer to people here in a couple of weeks than I had to people back home whom I had known for years. I would miss this feeling of community, this feeling of common purpose.

CHAPTER 8

Communicating with Spirits

DO I THINK EVERYBODY FEELS the spirits around them? Perhaps I feel more than most, but it seems like everybody at least senses that there are loving beings. People may not ordinarily sense who is there or know exactly how the spirits are working or what is happening on a spiritual level, but most people experience a very loving, protected feeling. I am feeling the spirits much closer here than I normally would back home. Is this because there is something special about this place and the amount of spiritual help here? Or is this because I am dedicating the time to listen, away from my busy life? Perhaps it's both.

In this special place in Brazil, whether they feel the spirits working on them or not, people are receiving this healing on a soul level. I realize now that this is the same healing energy that is present in ashrams in India or the mountains of Peru or quite simply your own backyard, if you are only open to it.

Dreams are, of course, one way that Spirit can communicate with us. Often people have more vivid dreams here in Abadiânia. I don't dream a lot usually, but I did dream after I had my spiritual surgery. These dreams were more vivid and real than normal, and they showed me lessons in my life, feelings that I should take notice of, and things that were going to change.

On one particular night, I just couldn't sleep. I suppose the time difference or jet lag makes it a little more difficult to fall asleep, but here at night sometimes the spiritual energy is so high. You feel excited, like a child waiting up all night for Santa, but in this case it was for no specific reason. This night the air was electric. The spirits felt so close, and I sat up conversing with them intently for hours. It was unlike any other spirit communication I'd ever had. This "session" felt so connected, it was just like I was sitting next to physical people, talking to them and asking them questions about the other side.

I felt like there was a whole panel of spirits and I was allowed and even encouraged to ask them questions. The answers were often profound and surprising. I wasn't making this up, was I? I couldn't possibly be. We had long discussions of karma, energy, spirits, past lives and lessons. I was asking my invisible friends, "What happens when somebody passes away? Where do they go? What happens to animals? Is everybody good? Are there negative spirits and how do we protect ourselves? What is Karma and what are life lessons?" We went deeper and deeper and I was enthralled. It was as real to me as my experience sitting here now, writing this book.

The spirits asked me to write everything down. I'm thinking, *"Believe me, I'll remember this! This makes sense. Now I understand, I couldn't possibly forget this. What you are sharing is revelatory to me!"* They assured me, "You won't remember, write it down."

I made copious notes that night, and they were right. In the morning I had a pile of incredible notes that I am still deciphering.

I can't even remember having written them. I only remember that the night occurred. What a wonderful experience to be able to sit and talk to the spirits and get answers! I didn't get answers about my life specifically—I didn't ask. They told me I really wouldn't care about the small details of my life, as we have free will to live the life we want.

I conversed with spirit all night until the sun came up. Then I realized what time it was and told them that I really needed to get some sleep because I had to get up in a couple of hours and go to the Casa. They said, "Don't worry. We will make it so you don't need sleep. You will feel completely refreshed." Shortly thereafter 7 AM rolled around. It was time to get up and get ready for the morning session at the Casa. I hadn't had one wink of sleep, yet I felt completely refreshed, as if I had slept like a baby.

I must have done this for two or three nights straight, staying up all night, and in the morning I knew I had a full night of conversation. I knew the gist of it but I couldn't recall specifics. It was like an intense dream you think you'll remember, but later that day you only know you had a vivid dream and you can't recall any details. I went to look at some of my notes, and I was astounded. *"Wow, I wrote this!"* I have pages and pages of these incredible conversations. One day I hope to decipher it all.

The other place where I was able to have many conversations with Spirit was in the current room. It is here that many people receive insights, communicate with Spirit, and may even receive their healings. Even those who don't normally feel spiritual presence often get messages. Most people at least experience the current as a very warm, loving feeling around them. Almost everyone senses that there is a very special energy in these rooms and a very nice vibration. Often it is just described as love. During the session, John of God is incorporated by one great, benevolent spirit, but at the same time there are hundreds of beautiful spirits healing through the energy of the current. If one is but a little sensitive, one can feel these beautiful souls.

The first time I went into the current room to meditate, it wasn't quite what I expected. From what others had told me, I thought I was just going to feel sleepy and experience a very warm, loving sensation. Actually, at first it was almost a little unnerving. I definitely could feel that there were hundreds of beautiful entities in the room working, but I was a little overly electrified by the high energy. It felt as if I'd had way too much caffeine. My body was over-sensitized to every little twitch and I felt edgy having to sit still.

I was seated next to one of the German guys from the group, and was trying to get in the flow and relax, but I was feeling out of sorts. I can feel spirit hands touching my face and I'm getting lots of messages all at once, but I feel almost hyper-energized and slightly uncomfortable. I'm trying to get into a calm rhythm, in sync with the flow, but I can't quite do it. The guy sitting next to me is clearly feeling the same way. I feel him shifting in his seat, moving around and almost jolting. He seems to be having a hard time going within. I receive an intuition and I reach over and grab his hand and just hold it. I concentrate on sending calming energy to him, at which point he instantly calms down and then together we finally get into the flow of the current. Afterward, he looked at me slightly embarrassed and whispered privately, "Thanks for holding my hand, I needed it." Nothing more was said.

These long meditation sessions are daunting. When meditating in the current room, you are told to keep your eyes shut the entire time and you aren't supposed to leave until the session is over. I'm wondering what happens if I need to go to the bathroom. Luckily, it never happened. Just keeping your eyes closed for that many hours, without even peeking, seems like it would be difficult. Yet sometimes you will be in there for hours and it feels like only twenty minutes. It feels like you could do it twice as long. It's not boring as you might think. There are lots of visuals and interaction with Spirit. It is the most wonderful feeling when you really get into the flow. This is the place where you can ask Spirit questions and you feel like you are receiving the answers.

My first time in current I asked, "Who is here? Who is sitting next to me? Who is touching me?" I sensed a beautiful lady sitting right next to me, a lady in spirit. She told me her name was Genovia. I don't know who she was but she had a 1920s feel, and a very feminine, very beautiful energy.

I connected with another spirit. The name St. Francis came to mind. I thought that it was totally my imagination, of course. Then, as I was thinking that, the piped music playing throughout the Casa switched songs and went to a beautiful Portuguese tune about St. Francis. I giggled to myself silently and said, *"Alright, maybe you really are there."*

Probably the most powerful spirit I felt in the current room was that of a Middle Eastern man. He had very strong, dark features and dark hair. I could only see his face. It was strong and powerful, yet benevolent. As I communicated with him telepathically, waves of love ran through me, not unlike an electric current. It was overwhelming and tears streamed down my face as I poured my appreciation back to him. When I asked, the name I got was "King Solomon." I knew that King Solomon had been known to work at the Casa, though it was rare. Again, I thought this was just my overactive imagination. But whoever this was, he was a charismatic and powerful spirit. As the Casa session ended and the people poured out of the current room, there was much excitement that this had been a very special session. For a short period of time, Medium João had been incorporated by the great spirit King Solomon!

CHAPTER 9

Spirit Healers

S O MANY HEALINGS take place during the Casa sessions—physical healings, spiritual healings, emotional healings. Many people come to heal severe diseases like cancer or because a physical ailment has left them crippled and unable to walk. There is actually a room at the Casa full of the discarded old wheelchairs and crutches that people no longer needed after being healed by the Entities.

Many times people are cured, but not always. Why is it that some get healed completely and some do not? Some say because it is not that person's karma to be healed, or it's not that person's real desire in their subconscious or higher self. Maybe they consciously think that they want to get well, but they're either not prepared to put in the effort or it's just not their life path. However, many people do receive miraculous healings and are returned to health. With some it is instantaneous and requires only the one visit. For others it requires several visits and changes to their lifestyle and way of thinking for completion.

Coming to the Casa is not just about physical healing, it's also about spiritual healing and continuing that path in your life. As a result, many of the people who have already been healed come back for a kind of tune-up or gratitude trip and to talk to the spirits in the current room. In fact, the more time I spent here, the more I realized that any physical healing is almost secondary.

Some say that the spirits are also working in a spiritual healing center above the Casa, set in an invisible tower that stretches up to the heavens and is for the purpose of healing those already in spirit. This may be a whole other dimension of healing going on, for one may think that when a person passes to the other side he or she automatically becomes an enlightened, all-knowing being. However, this is not true. Even spirits are continuing on their path and need continued healing.

Is there such a thing as negative entities? Well, I believe that negative or lower-energy spirits do exist; however, there is a lot of protection around the Casa. Reportedly the whole town is under a vortex or triangle set up by the Entities as an energy field of spiritual protection. Mediums and the other people at the Casa do play a role in continuing to draw in this beautiful positive energy. The healing spirits have set up this protective dome so that no negative energies can come within the boundaries. Very high, beautiful, benevolent spirits come through John of God, and you only feel beautiful energies when you are at the Casa.

Another way to talk to the spirits is to petition your requests to the "Triangle." At the back of the Casa stage hangs a wooden triangle where you can pray to the spirits and also place photos, names, or notes for you and your loved ones inside. This triangle is said to hold the energy of the Entities. People pray to the triangle by putting their hands on the sides and bowing their head inside the triangle to feel the spiritual energy and to talk to the Entities.

I had brought my email list of my spiritual clients in Los Angeles. I decided to put a copy of the entire list inside the triangle while I prayed, and I asked the spirits for healings for everybody on my list. Whatever they needed. Amazingly, when I got back home some of the people asked, "Did you do something on your trip at 10 AM on Thursday, Los Angeles time?" They felt the exact time I asked for the spirits to help them and experienced the energy of love at that very moment transmitting from Brazil. They reported things happening like "I felt this amazing energy" or "I received a check right at that time, and you have no idea how much I needed it" or "I had sprained my ankle and it was instantly better."

There is another healing triangle on the outer wall of the main Casa building that is dedicated to King Solomon. It is called the King Solomon Triangle. I found it to be a very pleasant place to just sit and meditate. One can also pray to that triangle, specifically communicating to King Solomon. On my second trip to the Casa, I sat in this area with my client, Collette. She had brought petitions from a few people back home who had requested healings. In particular, she brought one for the parents of a baby with Tay-Sachs, a rare and fatal genetic disease. Collette is collecting her thoughts on the petition she is placing in the King Solomon Triangle. I'm sitting next to her but not really in the zone, thinking more mundane thoughts. She asks me, "What shall I write about the Tay-Sachs baby?"

Before she writes anything, a sudden rush of intense energy comes down through me. It felt like a surge of electricity that entered through the top of my head and passed through my body, and I actually saw this energy connect to her piece of paper like a quick flash of light. I was completely overwhelmed. It was such an amazing feeling that I instantly burst into tears and was overcome by emotion.

She continued, "So what do you think I should put?"

Shaking and emotional, I said, "I think the healing already took place!" As she looked at my face, she could tell that something profound had just happened.

I felt somehow that I had been blessed to be a conductor of this amazing healing energy that passed right through me. I also received a message to give her. "From now on, don't say the child is a Tay-Sachs baby, but rather refer to the child by his name." The message was that we are not "the disease." We are the person currently experiencing the disease. This was an important point communicated to us—that we should never refer to somebody as "the cancer patient" or "the paraplegic," but rather to understand that person is an individual now enduring that illness.

I found the triangles to be such blessed connections to Spirit. Fortunately, you can buy a wooden triangle at the Casa that represents the spirits and the energy of the Casa. I purchased one and presented it to John of God. I asked the Entity to sign the triangle and to help me use it to transmit the energy at home. I believe that it was Dom Inácio who was incorporated at the time and who signed my triangle.

Inside my triangle, I placed a copy of a painting that hangs above the Entity's throne. It is of Dom Inácio, Jesus, and Mary. I feel adding this deepens that feeling of connection to the Casa. I bring the triangle to many of my events and invite people to come up to it. I invite them to put the names of their loved ones there and pray to the triangle just like they do in Brazil. People feel the energy. I am honored to have this blessing, and it's a wonderful way of connecting people to the energy of John of God and the Casa. I do believe that the spirits want to spread this energy around the world and want people to have this opportunity.

Another way to experience the energy is through the crystals. Many years ago, Medium João was told by the spirits that he should go to Abadiânia to buy a piece of land to build a healing center. What he didn't know at that time was why they chose Abadiânia. After he built the Casa, they discovered that the mountain it is situated on is a vortex of quartz crystals. João has mined some of the crystals that he carefully selects. Those crystals are sold at the shop, and that is how they support the Casa. This not only allows this amazing energy to travel around the world but the income allows the healings and the work of John of God to remain free to everybody. Quartz crystals are known to store positive energy so, as you can imagine, the crystals from the Casa are extremely powerful.

There is also a very special quartz crystal here they call "Medium Healing Crystals." Medium João selects these crystals from very deep down in the earth and they are actually formed with water inside the crystal. I had been told about these by another medium in Los Angeles. They are not advertised and you can't just go and buy them in the gift shop. They are meant for people that do healing work and are used for cleansing the healers themselves. You have to ask permission from the Entities to own a pair. In fact, when I inquired about them to one of the Casa guides, he looked at me carefully, took me to one side, and whispered as if I had discovered a top-secret password, asking me how I knew about these.

They were a considerable investment, so if I were to purchase some, I wanted to know not just that I had permission, but that they would actually do something for me. I went in front of John of God in Entity and I asked about the healing crystals. I asked if they would actually do anything for me, and if they would be powerful for me. The Entity said, "Yes, they would be very good for you. You should get them." And so, John of God picked a pair of special crystals for me. One is slightly larger than the other. They come as a pair, a male and a female. The female is shorter and fatter, and the male is longer and more phallic.... Go figure! I work with my healing crystals by holding them over my chakras and asking for that connection to the spirits in Brazil. I then ask for the crystals to cleanse my auras. It is important never to show these special healing crystals to anyone else. They are personal healing crystals, and no one else should look at them. I use them when I want to communicate with the spirits in Brazil.

Are these healing crystals very powerful and special? Well, I don't know. They feel very special to me. When I hold them, I feel their energy. I just need to hold them for a few seconds and I feel tremendous heat radiating from them that continues to generate energy for an hour or more. I also feel my "personal sign" that the spirits from Brazil are present: the fingertips on my temples. However, all the crystals from Brazil have an amazing energy.

I believe that if you dedicate this authority to your own pair of crystals and treat them as sacred living beings, that they become your special healing crystals.

I wanted to share this crystal energy with my spiritual group back home, and after getting permission I selected many small crystals. Actually, I stuffed my suitcase full of crystals! When I got to the airport my bag must have been about double the allowed weight. As I'm walking up to the counter, I tapped into the Entities and said, "Can you please help me? If these crystals are supposed to come home with me and they're meant for the people in my group, can you help me out here with the luggage?" I smiled at the attendant and greeted him. He noticed my English accent and started chatting about the time that he visited England. My monstrously heavy bag just went up on the belt without the attendant weighing it, and off it went without a peep.

When I presented them to my group there were just enough crystals for each person to have one. They were almost all gone that very night! People told me what amazing results they have received from these crystals. People felt that in holding them, they could feel the energy of the Casa. Many said when they held them in their hand, they actually felt shivers of electricity running up their arm. Quartz crystals are known for being powerful healers, but these crystals from this particular area, that have been blessed by the Entities and have resided at the Casa, have exceptional power.

CHAPTER 10

Talking to God

I'M NOW INTO THE second week of my trip and it is almost my birthday. I'm hoping the Entities will help me with a pressing issue that is weighing on my mind and is a big driving reason for my trip. Can they help me with the devastating legal issue that I have somehow inadvertently manifested in my life?

As has happened to me on more than one occasion, I have taken someone into my confidence, allowed them to become like family, and then gotten screwed over in the process. I'll spare you the grim details and simply say that this former friend and confidant, who worked for me, decided to sue me. It was a multi-million dollar, frivolous lawsuit. At first we didn't think it would go anywhere, it was such a transparent and obscene misrepresentation, but unfortunately a large law firm had sunk their teeth in and we were in for a serious fight. Not only was this a draining and frightening experience, but the betrayal I felt from someone I trusted made it all the worse. I knew there was some life lesson to be learned here, perhaps some karma between us, and I was trying my best to overcome my human instincts and to send her love and forgiveness.

The month before my trip to Brazil a court date had been set for the trial of this horrible lawsuit. You'll never guess—it was my birthday, December 16th! You have to be kidding me! How am I going to tell the court that an astrologer told me that if I am not in Brazil on my birthday, my life will be a disaster?

Despite my best excuses and pleading, the court would not budge on the trial date, but I was not going to change this trip for anything! So I left, believing that the judge would move the trial if I wasn't there. However, my attorney had advised me that there was a risk the judge would go ahead without me and I would lose by default, which would mean—oh, only about a three million dollar judgment against me! I figured that this would take me the rest of my life to pay off. Still, out of any date possible, this date had been chosen for a reason. I knew this couldn't be a simple coincidence. The Universe has some kind of plan and I am to trust. I am putting a lot of faith in Spirit!

Today I have slated my appearance in front of John of God to ask the spirits for advice on this desperate situation. All mortal means seemed to have led to a dead end, but I have faith in John of God. I have seen his miraculous healings, felt his divine connection, and I am sure that even in a business matter, the Entities could bring the angelic miracle I needed.

I am walking around the Casa gardens holding a brochure for my business and going over the best wording of the question to present. I am already putting the issue to the spirits so that they can have a good understanding of my situation. Spirit must have been listening, as almost immediately I got the message, "Go walk around the corner. Go hang out for a little bit, but don't go around the way you usually go. Walk around the other side."

I obediently do as I'm told. As I walk around the corner, a gust of wind comes out of nowhere and blows my brochure right out of my hand. Following it across the grass, I try to catch it, but each time it slips just out of my grasp. Finally the brochure lands. I run over and pick it up. I'm now right in front of a bench. *"Okay, I guess they want me to sit here for a while,"* I think. So I sit down on the bench, holding my brochure and contemplating the situation.

As I look up, I'm sitting right in front of a bust, a bronze statue. There are a few busts throughout the gardens, mostly of healing spirits that are known to help at the Casa. This one is a person in spirit, but it's a person that died more recently. It is of a man who was a friend of Medium João. He was born July 1st, 1916, and he died in 1982. This beautiful bust appears to be smiling down at me. I'm reading the inscription and it is later fully translated to me: Rivadávia Licinio de Miranda was an attorney general in life and now is a spirit for the justice of God.

I'm asking for help with a legal matter and here I have been put in front of a spirit, "an attorney for the justice of God." I got chills! I don't think I could get better legal advice than that! I feel a loving, protective energy in his smile, as if he is really smiling at me. Almost a knowing sly grin, like he's got a huge one-up on this case. He looks a bit like my own grandfather. Perhaps this is why he feels so friendly to me. Even more curious, his birthday is the same day as my grandfather's! I sit looking at this bronze bust, but it doesn't feel like cold metal; it feels like the presence of this wonderful man. I thank him with all my heart. I know this man in spirit is going to be my justice.

I hear over the Casa loudspeakers that my line has been called. I realize I need to hurry, and within moments it's my turn to go in front of John of God. I feel my issues are already being worked on; after all, I have already been assigned a spirit to help me. A spirit attorney, no less. But I still want to hear the words of wisdom from the great John of God himself. Perhaps through him I will receive heavenly guidance. As I place my brochure in front of him, I telepathically relay the entire information about my business. As I near John of God, I feel the overwhelming loving energy. Once again I am in complete awe. I believe this feeling never diminishes, no matter how many times one approaches. The sweet Entity incorporated today takes my brochure slowly and lovingly and says, "I will take it under consideration. Come back another time." I must admit I feel somewhat disappointed, as I was really hoping for a long explanation or at least an "everything will work out" reassurance. Though I know to be patient, as the spirits work in unexpected ways.

After you go in front of John of God, everybody is led, in small groups, through the current room and into a little recovery room for a closing meditation. A closing prayer is recited about being grateful to the spirits, first in Portuguese, then in English. I sit down in a pew and I close my eyes for this gratitude prayer. On this particular day I'm thinking, *"Well, I'm really just not in the zone. I should have meditated beforehand. I kind of got rushed in and, well, I'm really not in the place I should be."* I'm still busily thinking about my business and finances with my thoughts running riot through my head.

Then, in the middle of this busy mind-chatter, something happens to me—something so surprising, so unexpected, so profound. All of a sudden, out of nowhere, as if struck by lightning, a tremendous feeling comes over me. It is an indescribable, amazingly loving feeling that is consuming my very being. It's like a powerful column of bright white light that literally comes down from the ceiling and through my crown at the top of my head. In fact, my whole world is lit up. I actually feel the energy rushing in and filling up my heart, filling my chest fully and overflowing with the feeling of love. This is the only way I can describe it—just an intense feeling of love. I could compare it to being in love for the first time, but it was a hundred times stronger. So strong that I burst into tears of joy, tears that were gushing down my face. An overwhelmingly beautiful, emotional feeling, and so strong. I believe any stronger and my heart would have exploded.

As I'm experiencing this beautiful feeling of love, I'm completely pinned back against my seat—awe-struck, like I am physically unable to move, held in a beam of white light. I am in fact completely in awe, overwhelmed by the intensity of this emotion. I am crying tears of happiness, joy, and bliss that have overcome me. I am emotionally sobbing tears of absolute joy and appreciation.

Then I hear a man's voice, a deep, lovely, fatherly voice, beautiful and soothing. Now, in mediumship when I hear a message from spirit, it is more like a thought than an actual voice. This was not like a thought. This sounded like a person standing in the room next to me. This was an actual voice. This deep, comforting voice came over and said,

"But what is your higher purpose?"

The meaning that came to me with this statement was: "Why are you even caring about all these miniscule financial details? This is what you should strive for. This is where it's at. This is the feeling when you are in alignment. This is the energy. This is what your higher purpose is. This is what should be your concern, your passion. Everything else is meaningless."

I had a sudden sense of knowing that when you are in this place of glory, of love, of Divine connection, that everything else just either falls into place or disappears. It's not that important anymore. When you are in this place of Divine connection, everything works perfectly. So, if it's meant to be, it's meant to be, and it will be. To trust. What is most important is this connection. This is what it's about—this amazing, indescribable feeling! As I'm sitting here overwhelmed and completely pinned down, I stutter, "I want to share this with others. I want others to feel this feeling you are giving me."

The voice came back and said, **"So be it."**

My Divine bliss was interrupted when I heard the Casa volunteer say, "You can now open your eyes and leave."

I said to this voice in my head, "But I don't want to leave. I want to stay here!"

The same deep, comforting voice came back and said, **"My child, you can stay as long as you want."**

I sat through the whole of the next group meditation. I just sat in connection with this Divine presence, feeling one with God, one with love. I sat in awe, in perfect harmony as if the world had stopped; and, in that moment, my whole life changed and suddenly came together in one moment of knowing. What I experienced was beyond this world and beyond description. It was truly amazing.

And I swear that voice was the voice of God.

Never before had I heard or experienced that, and I really felt this was a direct connection with God.

I can only equate this to other people's descriptions of a near-death experience, where they've reported going to the other side, through the tunnel of white light, sensing an amazingly loving feeling, and then coming back to tell their story. Luckily I didn't need to have a near-death experience in order to have this connection.

I felt in that moment that I truly knew the work of John of God and the life that João had dedicated. This environment that he had created was all for the purpose of connecting each of us to God. Today I had really felt that connection. I had felt the devotion and I was eternally grateful to this beautiful saint, João Teixeira de Faria.

After I sat through the meditation twice, I figured I probably should let somebody else have a turn. So my physical side got the better of me and I got up and left. I walked out of there feeling like my life had completely changed forever—and it had. This miraculous event was only the beginning....

CHAPTER 11

Seven Pictures

TODAY IS MY BIRTHDAY. A lot revolves around this day. My astrologer told me that at the exact time that the stars will align in the same formation as my birth, I needed to be in my hotel room. I needed to be by myself and meditating on my birthday wishes for the year. I wasn't exactly alone. I had plenty of angelic watchers. As I put out my wishes for the year, I wanted a specific outcome on the lawsuit but I bit my lip and asked God to resolve everything for my highest and best interest. Anyway, I had already been given the most amazing birthday present anyone could ever imagine—connection to Source.

But I was still finding it difficult to trust. I craved confirmation. John of God in Entity had given me an invitation to come back and revisit the business issue. Today seemed like a great day to get some good news. Perhaps I would get some answers, specific direction, or just a reassurance that everything would be okay. I craved to feel the angelic blessing from John of God himself and knew that any words from him would come from the heart, from love, and those, I could absolutely trust.

When I had asked John of God the previous day about my business, it was Dom Inácio, a very sweet, kind, loving spirit.

Today is Dr. Augusto, who is known for being firm, very serious, and authoritative. His mannerisms are quick, abrupt, and business-like. When he is in charge, the line moves very quickly. Today I am getting this no-nonsense spirit.

I watch the people in front of me each get a quick diagnosis and be waved on expediently. When it's my turn, I once again take out my business brochure and with complete love and faith, ask John of God in Entity, "Can you help me with my business?"

All of a sudden the Entity, Dr. Augusto, stops the line, throws up his hands, and begins talking rapidly and very enthusiastically in Portuguese: bla, bla, bla, "muito importante...." He is going on and on. The translators are staring with open mouths. They've never seen anything like this. I don't understand a word, but I feel like I'm somehow getting a reprimand. The spirit doesn't sound very happy with me. I'm feeling a little awkward and thinking, *"Perhaps I didn't take my herbs when I was supposed to, or I did something else wrong. Whatever I've done, I'm in serious trouble here!"* The Spirit incorporated is pointing at my body and waving. The only thing I can understand is "muito importante." He is scribbling notes on a "prescription" pad next to him.

Spirit Dr. Augusto through John of God goes on for a good five minutes with the big tale about what should be done and how important it is. Finally he points to the side of him. "Sit here." I am told to meditate next to him.

As I sit down totally confused and a little humiliated, the translator whispers to me, "I need to see you afterwards, this is very important."

"What have I done?!"

The translator shoves the "prescription" in my hand. I sneak a peek at the paper. All I can make out is a number, the number 7. Everything else is in Portuguese spirit-doctor scribble. So now I'm sitting here, in the current room, next to the Entity. The session is going to last another two hours and I have no idea what I have done nor what this discussion was about. I just know I'm in serious trouble. All I can do, in this next two hours, is think about what can possibly be written on this piece of paper I am holding.

I'm meditating and meditating for what seems like an eternity, and finally the session is over. The translator is eager to find me. He tells me to come with him, that we have serious, important work.

"What? What did the Entity say?" I can hardly stand it.

"He said they are willing to help you, but they have got a lot of important energy work to do on you. It is of great importance to them that they do this work on you," he explains as he holds my hand, leading me in a hurry through the back rooms of the Casa. "We have to take seven photographs of you. But we've never done seven and I have to find out what to take." As he leads me through the Casa, everybody is looking at me like, "What happened?" "What did he say?" "What's going on?" "Why all the commotion?" Everybody was dying to know. As I'm being rushed through, I shrug my shoulders. "I don't know, I'm just having photographs taken."

I'm relieved that I don't seem to be in trouble and now, of course, I'm feeling extremely important. Today is my birthday. I think this is my birthday present. Everybody is running around, and finally there is a discussion with John of God in Entity and the

Casa manager. Basically they are to take pictures of my head, my Heart Chakra, above my head, full front and back, and some other angles—just regular photographs.

I am told that I have to come back in the morning, pick up my photographs, and present them to John of God in Entity for him to read the energy. I am also told that this very important energy work has already begun on me. As I leave the Casa, the suspense is killing me. I am dying to know what this is all about. I feel honored. The spirits are going above and beyond to help me, and it's something that they have deemed extremely important. I'm feeling very, very special!

That evening, my wonderful new friends arranged a little birthday party for me, a very nice surprise! We celebrate with flowers and some non-alcoholic champagne (I'm still on my forty days!). I'm very touched. We're having a nice time sharing lots of stories when suddenly, right in the middle of conversation, I feel my "signal" on my temples. This time it is extremely strong and has a sense of urgency. I suddenly feel extremely drowsy and have to lie down. Apparently I stood up, looked at everybody and said, "Okay, they're working on me. I gotta go. I gotta go lay down." I was later told that I was literally in mid-sentence when I stopped and announced that I was going to my room and left in a trance-like state. It was only 6 PM and in the middle of my own birthday party, but something much more important was occurring.

Major party pooper or not, I went to my room to lie down. The spirits were already working on me. It was extremely strong. I could feel a lot of beautiful energies working on me, a tingly feeling of electrical impulses directed over various areas of my body, as if spirit fingers were touching me. This continued for the whole evening and into the night until finally I fell asleep. I don't normally have vivid dreams or remember them, but that night I had some incredible dreams! They foretold much change.

The next morning is my big day for the spirits to read my seven photographs. I can hardly stand it, waiting to find out their meaning and significance. Of course everybody else at the Casa has by now heard about these seven photographs and they, too, are eager to hear what message they hold. I am given the photographs and they look like regular snapshots of me. There is nothing unusual that I can see, but I know that John of God and the Entities are going to be able to read their energy. I'm thrilled. I couldn't have asked for a more special birthday present.

As I stand in line, the anticipation is killing me. What magical secrets do these hold? Am I going to be helped by the spirits?

Today another Entity is incorporated. This one is much more calm, cool, and collected than Dr. Augusto yesterday. As I come in front of John of God, I sense a sweet, loving auric energy. As I hand my seven photos to the Entity, he looks at me and smiles sweetly. Without moving his gaze from my face, he takes the seven sacred photographs "for consideration" and gently drops them into a box next to his throne. He does this without even so much as glancing at them. Then he smiles sweetly and says a simple "thank you" as he looks to the next in line.

WHAT? WHAT? THAT'S IT? THAT'S ALL I'M GETTING?!!!

Where is the answer to my question? What am I going to do?

After all that fuss, this is it?! For the spirits to know and me to not find out?!!! Was this spirit not up to speed on what Dr. Augusto and his team were doing? Should I complain, take my photos back and ask when Dr. Augusto was seeing clients again? I was perturbed, to say the least.

But perhaps I wasn't supposed to know. After all, the work was already being done. Did I really need to know the how and the why? Or did I just need to trust? We, as human beings, always want to control. Was I trying to control not only the outcome but also how it was to be accomplished? Did I need to approve the next steps of the plan? Did I not completely trust this beautiful omniscient being? Later that day I sat quietly in the gardens and I put the question to Spirit. The answer that came was this: "This is not something we can just tell you an answer for. There will be many, many meetings and many things will happen. There will be guidance along the way. There is a higher purpose in this and a journey of self-discovery. You do not yet see the big picture." Not what I wanted to hear. What I wanted was, "All will be okay; we've taken care of it." However, I knew I was being worked on, and I knew that I would continue to get help back in Los Angeles.

Okay, you are dying to know what happened, and you'd like me to jump forward in the story. So, as I said, the trial was set for my birthday, the 16th of December. Surely with all this spiritual help, the judge would have taken pity on me and at least moved the date. I presumed that this would be my birthday present from Spirit. I checked my email and I do, in fact, have an email from my attorney. As I open it, I am expecting good news. I am expecting a postponement. The email reads, "Very sorry, I don't think the judge wanted to do this, but unfortunately because you were not present, he entered a default judgment."

My heart sank. The realization set in. I lost the lawsuit because I didn't show up, and I now have a multi-million dollar judgment over my head! Yet somehow, I knew that this was meant to be. Somehow I knew that there was something good in this seemingly grim outcome. It was difficult to see it amongst the bad but, subconsciously, I knew this was positive. "How could a multi-million dollar judgment against me be a positive thing?!" I argued with myself. I didn't really know.

My friends were waiting to hear the outcome at dinner and hoping a celebration was in order. When I broke the news everyone felt somehow that it would work out. This was something I should celebrate anyway. So that's what I did. I went out with my friends and we celebrated and then laughed about how crazy it was that we celebrated. We toasted with our non-alcoholic champagne and I threw up my arms to the spirits. By some means, they would sort it all out. I knew somehow this was going to be a wonderful blessing.

All would be revealed in due time, but we were right. As this unfolded over many months, I was given amazing spiritual protection. I had a spiritual attorney on my side as well as the miraculous power of John of God himself. In the end, I had to rearrange my life and my businesses and I learned that I had to be more careful with my trust. But ultimately I wasn't harmed in any significant way. Still, as I sat here in Brazil, not knowing the future, it was taking great effort for me to allow and have faith that it would all work out as it did.

I had only one day left in Brazil. I was sad to leave this miraculous healer, this human being that was so great, so powerful. I felt totally protected in his presence. I was also sad to leave my new friends. I felt I was leaving without completion. Some of my friends were still resolving their paths and I would miss seeing their daily developments. I was sad to leave the wonderful protective feeling, not only from the Casa but from the people whose lives had touched mine. I was also almost a little afraid to go home and face all the changes I knew spiritually were coming.

My last session at the Casa I said my goodbyes to the Casa staff, the volunteers, and all the wonderful people I had met. Then with profound gratitude, I said goodbye to the person who had changed my life forever, Medium João, and to John of God in Entity. I had three requests to the Entity before I left:

Can I write this book?

Can I bring people here?

Can I make a film about you?

I was given a huge blessing on all three. "Of course you can and you will."

CHAPTER 12

Back from Brazil

IN CALIFORNIA once again, I'm feeling like I have undergone a crash course in spiritual growth, having received considerably more insights than I could have ever foreseen, even in my wildest dreams. I had met a living angel who has opened my heart and changed my life path. I am still processing and integrating it all, but I know one thing for sure—I want to share these incredible revelations with my Monday night Spirit Social group. I want everyone to know of this beautiful phenomenon, John of God. I send out a very basic email, something like "Hi, I'm back from Brazil. I have photographs and I'm going to give a little talk about my experiences, so come on down to my house." I attach a few photos.

I'm expecting to have a small group of maybe twenty people. Not even five minutes go by and I get a phone call. A woman from my group says, "I don't know what happened, but I opened your email and it was like this white light came down from above my head, through my body, and into my heart. I was completely filled with this intense feeling of love." She goes on excitedly, "I was so overwhelmed with emotion that I just started crying with happiness. I don't know what it was, but it had to do with your email. I got this amazing feeling of love from it."

"But it gets better!" she continues in complete awe and disbelief. "I forwarded it to my aunt, who doesn't really believe in any of this. Well, my aunt called me immediately and said she opened the email and all of a sudden felt this amazing white light, like she was just bowled over with love, and just got this amazing feeling."

As she is saying this I'm thinking, *"Really...? Is it really possible?"*

At first it didn't make sense to me. I didn't say anything significant in this email—basically just I'm back, I've got pictures, come down and see me. A few minutes later I got an email from someone else saying, "I just received your email. I've had this back pain. It's bothered me for years, and when I opened your email, I got this wonderful feeling and all of a sudden my back stopped hurting. I just feel fantastic. I don't know what was in your email but I'm coming to your event."

Then another.... "Wow, I just opened your email and I got this awesome feeling. Later when I went to the mailbox, a check that I have been waiting for, for months and months, finally arrived. Since I got your email today, everything seems to be going great."

All day long I'm getting phone calls and emails of similar stories. I thought, *"Can this be true?"* Had this energy somehow traveled on its own through my email? It seemed crazy, but so many people came to me with stories of receiving a wonderful energy. I think back to that surgery room where I had my profound experience. Where I talked to God. I remember my words, my request.

"I want to share this energy with others."

I humbly wonder, *"Really, is it really possible?"*

Monday night rolled around, and I could not believe how many people showed up at my house. There had to be over a hundred people. There wasn't enough parking, but somehow we crammed everybody in. I was so honored. Everyone was saying something similar. They felt an amazing energy. They received a physical healing. They manifested something wonderful.

"How could this be?"

I put together a little slide show and I talked about my experiences in Brazil. I spoke passionately about this miraculous healer and told of his angelic energy and loving presence. I told everyone about the current room where people meditate during John of God's healing sessions. I told them we were going to do a little meditation and to pretend that we are in the current room. I'm going to ask the spirits from Brazil if they would like to join us tonight. As I started the meditation, I explained something that had happened to me in the current room, something the spirits had taught me down there. It went something like this:

"Think about when somebody does something nice for you or when you feel love from someone. Somebody smiles at you, in some way makes you feel loved, hugs you, or sends you a little message of caring. How warm and wonderful you feel. It feels like waves of warm fuzziness. You feel it is being sent to you and received by you. This is what it feels like when someone sends you love."

I explained it as it had been explained to me by the spirits in Brazil. It's something that to me was a great revelation, that I believe is of upmost importance. Something that is available to us, and we do it automatically, we just don't realize it:

"When you love somebody else that energy comes down through the top of your head and down into your heart, filling up *your* heart first. It comes in from God, from Divine Source, and it comes down through your crown and then into your body. It fills up your heart until you feel amazing. It spreads through your body, and when you are completely full of love then this love overflows, flowing out from your heart to the other person."

"This happens when we simply smile at somebody, when we do a little nice gesture for somebody, when we think kindly of them, and of course when we intend to actually send somebody love. So, in order for us to send love to somebody, we have to receive that love first. It happens automatically, all the time. That love flows into us, through us, and fills us. If we are giving that energy of love, we first must have that energy of love to give. It has to come from somewhere, and it comes from God."

Basically, when we love somebody else, we have to love ourselves first. So when we want to receive a healing, when we want to receive something nice in our life, when we want to feel loved, we shouldn't be looking externally. We should not be asking "What can they do for me?" or "I want that person to love me," but rather "Who can I send love to?" Because when I send love to somebody, I have to receive it myself. I have to open up and allow that love to come in to me first.

Sending love gives us a hundred times greater love energy than if we just receive it from someone else. When we place ourselves in this love energy by asking to love another, we allow it to come into us; we are allowing healing energy to flow through us. This healing energy is God energy, which is pure unconditional love. So if we want healing in our lives—physical healing, emotional healing—if we want to manifest wonderful things in our lives, if we want happiness, joy, and prosperity, we should place ourselves in this flow of beautiful unconditional love. The absolute best and easiest way to do this is simply to love another.

It is when we place ourselves in this beautiful energy of pure unconditional love and allow this energy to flow through us that the spirits who love and assist us are able to channel through us, come close to us, and to help clear our aura and illuminate our spiritual bodies. We are attracting their energy to us because we are lighting up our souls and attracting energy of the same vibration.

It is this opening up, this allowing love to flow through us, that is our connection to Divine Source, our connection to God.

The spirits told me that it is not they that heal. It is not they that manifest things in our lives. The spirits can guide us but the actual healing force is God's love. It is this pure connection and flow of energy from God to us. It is everyone's birthright. We are supposed to be in alignment with this amazing energy. We are supposed to be connected to God, to pure unconditional love. This is what it feels like when we are on our true path. This is our right to feel this way. In fact, we are a part of God. We are, each and every one of us, at the core level, God. That is, we are, at the soul level, pure unconditional love. When we are open to being connected in this way the spirits can guide us into that connection, to make it stronger, to put us on our path; but when we feel that indescribable feeling of immense love, that is truly our connection to God.

I know it is impossible to feel and act like this most of the time, but the more you can live your life smiling at people in the supermarket, making the effort to care and spend time with the people you love, adding those extra little nice gestures, and generally thinking about and helping others, the more you bring love to yourself, and the more your life will move happily and prosperously in the right direction.

Putting ourselves in a meditative state where we are feeling love actually allows benevolent spirits to be able to help us more easily. If we are experiencing love, our negative ties and attachments are loosened, and the spirits are able to help us release that negative energy.

As I continue this meditation, I ask each person to concentrate on a time in their life when they really felt loved: "Think of a time when you really felt that energy. Whether it was your birthday party when you were a kid, or playing with your puppy, or holding your child, or the feeling of being in love romantically. Think of any one time in your life. We are not trying to find the greatest moment or the strongest—that doesn't matter. Just a time you can remember when you felt love."

I then asked everyone to recreate that feeling by recalling and really delving into every detail of that experience in order to make it stronger and stronger. I told them that if their imagination jumped around trying to find the perfect moment, not to worry about it, but to settle on any moment. I also cautioned them not to bring up an event with mixed emotions, such as a wonderful romance that they know later caused pain and suffering. What we were looking for here was any little moment of pure, uncomplicated love.

It is a known scientific fact that if you can imagine something with enough detail and conviction, your subconscious does not know the difference between the actual event occurring or it just occurring in your imagination. Therefore, if you can recreate that loving memory with enough conviction, you can actually bring that love into your being, just as you would if it were happening all over again. As I guided everyone through this exercise, they were really doing this. They were opening up and allowing that energy, right there and then, to come down through their crown and into their heart, feeling it grow stronger and stronger.

At this point, I asked the spirits from Brazil and any other benevolent spirits and angels that wanted to work with us to come into our auras. All of a sudden there was a very powerful feeling of loving beings descending into our room. You could feel the environment, the energy around us, rising to a new vibrational high. It was as if a massive influx of pure love had just surrounded us, as if you were caught up in the wave of an operatic story that suddenly moved to a new crescendo and brought you to an emotional high where you couldn't help but release your tears. It was as if you were in love for the first time, your heart bursting with overwhelming joy, but ten times greater.

Each person felt a dramatic, powerful surge of love in their heart. You could see that people were filled with emotion, and many were openly moved, bursting into tears of joy and love. There wasn't a dry eye in the room.

Everyone was now in a euphoric state, surrounded by loving healing spirits and truly connected. It also seemed that having a group of people doing this in unison somehow multiplied the effect, not by the number of people but many times more—as if there were a group resonance or entrainment effect where the vibrational high of one carried the energy of the others to a higher level. Now, with each and every person filled with overflowing love, I asked them to send out that love. "Send love to your loved ones at home, send love to those that are in spirit, send love to the person next to you that you don't even know, and if you are really, really brave, send love to those you dislike, to your worst enemy."

I could see in this heightened state of vibration that people's spirit guides and angels were also receiving this healing, this energy. These beautiful beings were around each and every person, as well as their loved ones in spirit. I took this opportunity to guide everyone to talk with their own loved ones and to be open to hearing them. This was a time when people could easily reach out and connect with their loved ones on the other side and many reportedly did.

I was told by Spirit to physically touch each person and to be a human conductor of this energy. As I walked around the room and placed my hand on their head, their heart, or their shoulders, I could feel the transfer of loving energy, like waves running through me. People responded with more overwhelming emotion, like they had felt and received a surge of love.

I cannot say that I was channeling spirits. I was quite aware of my physical body and I didn't, at any point, leave. People were connecting on their own and receiving this direct connection with

Divine Source, with God. They were doing this for themselves. There were beautiful spirits working with each of them.

I was no guru, no healer. I was just somehow blessed to be the facilitator of this event.

People came up and hugged me, blown away by the emotion they felt. Some tried to express their gratitude and the depth of feeling, but no words were necessary. I had felt it too. Some told me of the instant physical healing that they had just received: a lady with a third-degree burn suddenly healed; neck and back pain disappeared. All present that night received a healing from a soul level. An emotional healing, healing of physical ailments that hadn't even manifested yet, and an emotional well-being. More importantly, they themselves had done this, and I knew somehow that this connection was theirs forever.

Those who brought photographs of their loved ones, or even thought about them, felt that these loved ones had been touched too. Not only had we touched the hundred or so people that came that night, but hundreds more through the photographs of friends and friends of friends. This beautiful evening was a true turning point for me. At the time it was the biggest impact I had ever imparted on a group.

CHAPTER 13

An Urgent Return

AFTER MY JOHN OF GOD TALK and meditation that night, I started to get a flood of emails from people talking about this amazing energy. It was not only what they felt that evening—people were now saying they felt as if they remained connected to this energy. That somehow this night had put them in touch with this energy directly. Perhaps John of God had touched their lives even from thousands of miles away. As the days went by, they were continuing to have this feeling and were manifesting amazing things in their life: wonderful changes and positive events. I was told the most moving stories about how their lives had completely turned around. I knew that this was a very special time, a very special energy.

Many people wanted to go to the Casa themselves and experience this amazing energy. They wanted to meet this living saint, this human being with not only extraordinary abilities, but also a heart that felt like God's love. I was already putting together a group and had several people excited to go. It would take some planning. People needed visas, time to prepare, and of course they need the funds for this long journey. I knew that those who wanted to go would be provided for somehow. However, I was stunned at how people were receiving this energy right here, without even making the trip to Brazil. They had felt it.

I wanted to share this experience, this energy, with as many people as possible, not just my little group. I knew that if people could receive the energy simply from an email, then if I filmed in Brazil or wrote about this beautiful person, John of God, it was possible that the energy could travel through those mediums as well. It could travel through television, film, the spoken word, and perhaps even this book....

I had this secret wish that this would be my mission. That I would be able to bring what I had felt and what I had experienced to many, many people.

I called my friend Liz, a filmmaker, and told her that we have to shoot John of God in Brazil, this is just too amazing not to. "This man is a walking, living saint whose presence needs to be known in every corner of the world," I affirm. Liz said she was thrilled and would love to go to Brazil. I was thinking of a trip in a few months, also taking clients from my group. However, Liz was booked on a film starting in three weeks that would tie up her schedule for several months. We decided we would go to Brazil immediately and film.

Shortly thereafter, Liz and I sat down and talked about the finer details of shooting John of God. I had already asked permission from John of God and the Entities on my first trip to film, but we knew we would have to please them. Actually, we had to please them all: the Casa managers, the Entities, and Medium João.

We discussed what shots we were going to try to capture and

how I would interview people to bring across the proper message. We talked about how many filmmakers who go to Brazil concentrate on the physical surgeries. People tend to be sensationalistic and focus on things like "The Thing-Up-the-Nose Surgery" and cutting people's abdomens open. There are multiple documentaries on the miraculous psychic surgery: "Is this fake? Is this real?" Or "how could he do these physical surgeries with no anesthesia?" We didn't want to repeat what everybody else had done. My sense from being there was, yes, these physical healings are amazing and spectacular; however, everybody there gets a spiritual healing. I knew that this subtle spiritual healing is far more important than the physical healings. There is spiritual enlightenment happening. There is a spiritual connection, and this is a place on Earth where people can go to get connected. People need to know about John of God, his message of love, his beautiful heart, and the possibilities that he gives to all.

John of God's spiritual healing center is a very special place with a very special energy. How can we best reveal this to an audience? How can I bring across what I was sensing and feeling there, as well as my personal experiences? How can we show the powerful spiritual healing I received? How can we show the profound spiritual opening that happened for me? That's what we really want to capture: to bring across the spiritual enlightenment, the opening of the people to God Source energy. To show physical healings, but also mental healing and spiritual well-being. To show how one's journey here is potentially life-changing and how the experience can be used to manifest a better life. To be on one's soul purpose. As we discussed this, I said, "Well, how are we going to present that? What shall we say is the theme?"

Liz casually said, "Sounds like we should just ask the Entities to direct it." At that very moment the lights in the house dimmed down and then went back up again. We were like, "Okay, I guess that's our answer—just let the Entities direct it!"

So only a couple of weeks later, much sooner than I had expected, here I was headed to Brazil again. Had the spirits given me another excuse to get back this soon? I had one brave, spontaneous client who managed to pull it all together on the short notice and join us. We had many more supporters back home who came with us in spirit, waiting to feel the energy when I placed their blessings in Brazil.

Right before we left, I was invited to see the Iveron Icon that was in town visiting from Hawaii. The Iveron Icon is a small painting of Jesus and the Virgin Mary that reportedly gives miraculous healing to those who visit it. What is most miraculous is that when people pray to the Icon, it weeps myrrh oil that smells like sweet roses. I had been given permission to bring Liz along to film, and had been granted an interview with the priest. I experienced the phenomenon first-hand and had been allowed to hold this Icon as it did indeed weep oil all over my hands!

Then we were off to Brazil. As the airplane wheels touched the runway on our landing, Liz and I looked at each other in amazement. There was an unmistakable sweet smell of roses! Our trip was surely to be a blessed one.

CHAPTER 14

My Mission

AS WE ARRIVED in Abadiânia, a warm familiar feeling came over me. I felt at home once again. I felt like I belonged here.

The first order of business was to get permission to actually film! Of course, I had already asked the Entity a few weeks before, but you still need to ask on the actual day of filming. First we have to go in front of John of God while he is incorporated with a spirit and ask that Entity for permission to film. Then, if we get a positive response from the Entity, we need to ask Medium João. Finally, we have to ask the Casa managers.

Our trip comes in the wake of the airing of Oprah's episode about John of God. Given the reach of Oprah, it seems that word is out more than ever. Film crews have become a regular fixture at the Casa. This is becoming a bit overwhelming for Medium João, who has cameras in his face all the time. We've been told that Entity is being a bit touchy about cameras in his current room and wants the amount of filming reduced. There are already a couple of other crews here, professional crews with several cameramen running around. Then there is little old me, Liz, and our one small, inconspicuous camera.

All we can do is hope for the best. We get in line just like everyone who is there for a healing from John of God, but our request is for permission to film. Liz and Spikey, whom we've co-opted to be our local partner in crime, stand beside me. When it's our turn, the translator whispers in the Entity's ear, relaying our request in Portuguese. John of God is not taking much notice of the translator; he already knows our question. He looks at us in a warm loving manner. He takes my hand and smiles. The beautiful energy that seems to flow from his heart and over your being is a blessing in itself, but his words are translated by a stunned guide:

**"The message of your film is the most beautiful
I've heard in thirty-three years.
Of course you can film."**

Had we heard correctly? I'm overwhelmed by the answer. I never dreamed we'd receive such a blessed response. Even the translators were looking at us in amazement. I could imagine them thinking, *who are these people who've just been told that their film will be the most beautiful in 33 years!?* They were awestruck as well.

Usually the answer to a request to film is a simple yes or no. More recently, the answer has been a reluctant yes or an irritated no. But today, Spirit is welcoming us with open arms, telling us that the message of our film is beautiful. We had talked about allowing the Entities to lead us in the storytelling, but we never told this to anyone. The only thing that was told to John of God was simply that we wanted permission to film.

With such an overwhelming welcome from the Entity, the

Casa management had no problem giving us the green light as well. The red carpet was rolled out, and we were given the VIP treatment. We could film inside the Entity's current room, the physical surgeries on the stage, wherever we wanted. We were even invited to interview Anabelle, who has been paralyzed since she was a toddler. Oprah's crew had wanted to interview this young girl but hadn't been able to get permission. Somehow, we were. I'd been hoping for merely a yes to our filming and here we'd been given one of the most amazing responses anyone had received from the Entity.

We started filming right away, at the very next session that afternoon. I was to go back in front of John of God with my healing request. Liz was allowed to film in the current room, standing near John of God in Entity and filming the people as they came up to him to present their healing requests. I was standing in line, slowly making my way through the current room. As I stood in this current, I thanked the spirits over and over for this deep blessing and to have been chosen by the Entities to deliver a message to the world, directed in their way. I felt the golden waves of love, peace, and acceptance passing over me. I had been given the ultimate acceptance and I wanted to pour my heart out in gratitude.

The length of time it took to make one's way through this long line wasn't an irritation. It was the exact opposite. Standing in this line was like standing in the arms of God. Standing in this line was an experience of being held and caressed by angels and healing beings. It was a great healing in and of itself. I was not waiting in line to be attended to, but rather I was receiving miracles along the way. I cherished every step walking in this energy.

In my hand I clutched a scrap of paper with nearly a thousand names from my group back in Los Angeles—the names of people for whom I was requesting a blessing. I ran through my mind thoughts of specific people on the list and the difficulties that I knew they were having. I knew each and every person on that list was being guided and healed; whether I knew them and their issues or not, it had already been done. I didn't need to be specific—the thought had gone out long before this moment and the work was instantaneous. I knew just in the asking would come the healing.

More than anything, I stood in line to give back my gratitude. To ask, "What can I do?" I knew words were not needed to communicate with this spiritual world, but I wanted to give them anyway. Thank you for welcoming us, thank you for allowing us to film, thank you for such a gracious welcome. How can I share the love that I have received from you? How can I give back what little I have to offer in comparison?

It's now my turn to be seen. The Entity smiles, the kind of smile where love passes like a tangible wave connecting one heart to another. He holds out his hand to touch mine. I drop to my knees, overpowered by this majestic energy. An aura that surrounds him is now overlapping mine, and I gently kiss his hand. I mouth the words "Thank you" but the feeling is far deeper, like my heart is open and raw, pouring out all that a mortal person can. I wish that I had more to give. A moment that was probably a mere five seconds has an impact of a lifetime. My feelings were acknowledged in an unspoken communication.

I was gently guided off through the little surgery room, now my favorite room in the whole world. This offered me a few minutes to gather thoughts and cherish the energy before going about the day. Now I get to sit here, once again, for a few moments and communicate with Spirit.

I listen to the Casa guide giving a closing meditation, not understanding one word of Portuguese, but being carried away by the melody of this beautiful language. I sit in gratitude, thanking the spirits for this welcome; thanking them for knowing my sincerity; thanking them for the opportunity to serve and pass the message to others. Suddenly a deep, overwhelming feeling comes down through my crown and into my heart. This beautiful, expanding feeling of love that I had felt so strongly in this very same place and tried so many times to recreate with only a smidgen of result, I now felt once again. As the energy came in, I felt it building and building, expanding my chest until it was so bright that I thought I was going to burst. My eyes welled up and overflowed with joyful tears. *"Oh God, thank you"* was about all I could say silently in my head, as even in my mind I was speechless. "Just feel this connection. Feel this love" was the message I was getting. I was now surrounded by light beings. I couldn't see them but I could sense them. Then it came, a deep but warm and loving voice, as real as mine or yours.

"Do you accept this mission?"

This sounded so awe-inspiring, how could I not be thrilled that such an honor had been placed upon me? Yet something told me it might not be as easily accomplished as one might think. I felt that perhaps I wasn't saintly enough for such a grandiose spiritual mission. Surely they must know this. I replied tentatively, "Yeah, I think so." A rush of warm, comforting love was sent to reassure me. Then I was given a last-chance warning to reconsider if I wanted to back out gracefully.

"Relationships will change. Many people in your life will change. Things will not stay the same. Are you sure, are you ready for this?"

Somehow I knew change was an inevitable part of this equation. I suspected that one of those people was probably going to be my husband. I was shown images, somewhat like a fast-forward video of the many changes to come in my life. I caught only glimpses of these people that were to come and go. I didn't see the specifics of whom or how, so much as I saw the energies that I would draw to me and the energies I would no longer allow around me. I knew that this path would not always be easy. Some of my old habits would be hard to give up, but I knew this was my calling.

Again the voice asked the question, "Are you willing to accept this mission?"

This time I gave a definite "YES!" with tears running down my face. I was in a state of surrender and willing to accept everything I would encounter in this effort. Knowing that there was nothing to fear and that I would be shown the way, I didn't need to worry. I didn't need to ask for anything. I would be in the flow. I would be in this energy. This was my soul purpose. This was my path, and in living it I would be guided because this is my true purpose in life.

I walked out into the Brazilian sunshine. My face was streaked with tears of happiness and a huge smile. I knew that this was a complete change in my life and that there were many more changes to come, but this was the right path. This was *my* path.

CHAPTER 15

Love Is in the Air

I T'S 8 AM AT THE CASA, a time of bustling activity as everyone gathers for the day. People are exchanging their morning
greetings, chatting excitedly, and preparing for the morning
session. I'm with Liz and Spikey getting ready to film and going
over our goals for the day. Something draws my eye to the Casa
café and I notice a man gazing at me, the morning sunshine
streaking across his face. I immediately find him very attractive,
but I can't put my finger on what exactly it is about him. Presence
perhaps? I remember thinking that men should wear white more
often. The Banana Republic casual chic look is very becoming.
I'm drawn to him, tingling with excitement, but intrigued as to
why he is attracting my attention so strongly. He's clearly been
watching me a while. I give a shy smile and he smiles back with
confidence. There is a moment between us, one of those where
sparks go off and there is a silent acknowledgement going back and
forth. Perhaps it's soul recognition or perhaps it's just two people
noticing a physical attraction. I broke the gaze, looking down and
chuckling like a teenager. I didn't know who he was.

I am snapped back to reality as we strategize about the day
ahead. It's decided that I will go in front of John of God and present

photos from my group back home. We've been given permission to have the camera next to John of God and film the entire session, so Liz will include me in frame as I approach with requests to the Entity.

Spikey, who had left, rejoins us and tells me that the guy from the *Healing* movie wants to meet me. I was eager to meet him as well. During my first trip to Brazil, I had heard about *Healing*, a documentary about John of God that people were raving about. There were posters at the Casa showing that it had won awards at film festivals. People who had seen the film talked about how it was the most incredible and beautiful portrayal of John of God. I was excited to see it, but I was concerned that if it were about to be released in the United States, it would be a competing project.

Back home in California I had tried unsuccessfully to find a copy of the movie for research. You couldn't order it anywhere. Surely, I thought, here in Brazil I could buy a copy. However, when I inquired at the Casa, they explained that they were still waiting to get copies themselves. A thousand copies of the DVD had been sent to the Casa but had been stopped in customs. The only copies of the movie had been sitting in customs for six months!

I wondered what was going on. Why were the Entities not allowing this movie to get out? Some spiritual intervention had to be going on here. Still, this movie could potentially be our biggest competitor. The less angelic side of me wasn't unhappy to hear its dilemma. So, apparently a producer from the *Healing* movie, Josef, is here at the Casa today and would like to be introduced to me. It's nice to know whom we are up against! I feel a bit intimidated but I am excited to meet Josef and learn the real deal about this mystery film.

To my surprise, Spikey brings over the man I had shared a little moment with earlier. Josef sits down and we immediately hit it off. He's from Austria and has a charming German accent, a sweet, softer version of Arnold. *"An added layer of charm,"* I think. I explain that we're here doing a documentary. Josef shares his involvement with the film *Healing*. He was part of the production team and had put the project together. Josef is now preparing for his upcoming live event, John of God visiting Vienna to perform healings. He is at the Casa this week shooting promotional footage and appears to have quite a team of filmmakers running around the grounds under his direction.

Right away, Josef offers to help. He has some original footage of Medium João as a young man that we can use. He offers to show us the ropes and help us out with any of the idiosyncrasies of shooting at the Casa. Liz and I exchange glances in bemused excitement. Wow, this guy is rolling out the red carpet for us here and he's the big competition, so we think. Bluntly I ask the burning question. "So I've heard that this movie has not been distributed. I can't get a copy anywhere. What is the deal? Why are the Spirits not allowing it out?" Josef smiles and says, "Oh yeah. I guess you figured it out."

It seems that after the film won awards and was getting recognition, egos flared up amongst the filmmakers and some people lost sight of the message in the movie. Josef left the project. Now this beautiful film appears destined to get little exposure.

Josef expressed that it was very important to keep integrity when working with this energy. These were words of caution I would very much take to heart.

We got to hear Josef's incredible story of how he became involved with John of God; how he came to Brazil as a disbeliever, simply as support for his uncle who was gravely ill and looking for a cure. Like most, Josef went through miraculous discoveries that completely changed his life. The first was a healing story similar to many I'd heard. Josef had an old soccer injury on his leg. On his first day at the Casa, his leg was bothering him and one of the Casa mediums offered to pour blessed water on his old wound. Josef couldn't imagine that even the holiest of water could do anything. More out of politeness than anything else, Josef gracefully accepted. To his amazement, a large surgery scar on his leg disappeared instantly before his very eyes.

The next story is a little stranger than most, though again, many reports from the Casa leave one bewildered. Josef was hanging out on the benches waiting for his uncle when one of the ladies suggested that he go to the triangle and pray. He didn't put much stock in it, but figured why not? So he placed his arms on the triangle and bowed his head like he had seen others do. Within a second, there was a tap on his shoulder. He turned around to see who was disturbing him. There beside him was the last person he would have expected to see in this small rural town in Brazil. There was his best friend of many years. His friend told him this was a wonderful place to be. The crazy thing was, his friend had died the year previously!

Apparently as the color left Josef's face upon seeing this vision, he staggered backwards as if he were about to pass out. As he sat down, he was pouring sweat. Friends ran to his aid but he didn't explain why he suddenly felt faint. It was some time before he could process this and talk about it.

Josef had been a very successful artist for many years, sought after for his landscape paintings, which were sold through Sotheby's. After being involved with the Entities and John of God, he started painting pictures of the spirits and healers at the Casa, such as Dom Inácio, Jesus, Mary, and Medium João/John of God. Josef had no idea the energy that he was channeling through his art. He was shocked when people reported miraculous healings just by sitting in front of his paintings. His line of special energy paintings became known as "Healing Pictures."

We get some insight about Medium João as a person, his personal life, and also an amusing description of preparing for a John of God live event. Apparently Medium João does not switch off so easily. Dealing with João, who according to Josef is ninety percent of the time incorporated with Spirit, is like talking to a different person daily. Traveling so close to João sounded like a blessed position to be in. Apparently it could also be exhausting. You see, João doesn't seem to ever sleep. Perhaps João gets his sleep while spirits take turns incorporating his physical body. The spirits also kept Josef awake for five days straight as different spirits came in and out for their shifts and imparted their words of wisdom. So Josef had to converse with one spirit incorporated at perhaps 1 AM and maybe another later at 3 AM and with yet another spirit at 5 AM.

Liz and Spikey go about their way. Josef and I are left, enthralled in conversation for hours, looking deep into each other's eyes and knowing that there is some further connection than just two spiritual filmmakers sharing stories.

Afterwards Liz whispers in my ear, "I think he fancies you and he wants to give you footage! I'm serious, he likes you, now don't blow it!" she warns sternly.

"Yes, mom," I reply. Did she not pick up that it might be mutual?

Our long conversation continued into the days ahead, Josef and I hanging out in between filming takes, pretending not to flirt. He with his multi-man crew, who checked in with him periodically. Me with my two-man team: Liz and her camcorder, and our helper Spikey. Josef kept asking me, "So when is your film crew coming down?" I'm thinking, *"This is it"* but didn't want to tell him that. I told him we planned to come back in a couple of months, which was true. But probably with only one or two people again, which I conveniently failed to mention. Still, I was confident that we were also getting beautiful footage having just been given *carte blanche* from the Casa and from the Entities, no less, to film what was about to be the most beautiful message in thirty-three years!

Every free moment, Josef and I would find each other and chat. I'd often come across him surreptitiously looking around for me. His face would light up as he caught sight of me, and he'd put on a nonchalant, "Oh, I happened to notice you and thought I'd wander over" look. Sometimes I'd glance over and catch him staring at me. He'd probably been watching for some time. I felt a little self-conscious at being the subject of his voyeurism but giggly inside that

I was being pursued.

This underlying current, this flirtatious attraction, consumed me for most of the rest of the trip. When two people connect so strongly, so instantly, is it a past-life recognition? Is it chemistry? Is it simply physical attraction? We connected. We got to know an awful lot about each other in such a short time. We must have had a lot of time between filming takes! Or was it his charming way of getting me to share the most intimate of details.

I realized his interest in me was not to be subtle when the first day he looked at my wedding ring and said, "So, what's the deal? Are you married?" Yes, I was married. Things had not been good for quite some time. I'd spent the last year oscillating between the fear of how bad a divorce could be and thoughts of perhaps it was possible to breathe some life into the few moments of civility we had left. I knew I was living in an unhealthy, negative environment, walking on eggshells and staying out of his way, hoping he'd be in a better mood later. Fear was what was really holding me there, including fear of a very acrimonious divorce. I chose to gloss over the day-to-day snide remarks. I was too scared of change, so it was easier just to put up with it and put on a smile.

Though I put the blame pretty much on myself. You see, he had been the right person for me at the time. I was the one who changed. He was the very same person I was excited about and attracted to nine years earlier. At the time I was obsessed, as well, with the chase of business deals, power, more stuff, more money. Like attracts like, and my husband was just the right energy for me.

My contact with spirituality had changed my life, a complete

180. My life values had changed. I wanted to enjoy life more. Not that I had gone all woo-woo or anything, just subtle changes that were not noticeable to most. Of course, I still cared about my businesses and having enough money, but I cared less about the chase of money and more about enjoying the now. Where was his high-rolling business wife bringing in the ace deals? Where was the person he could get enthusiastic with about the next deal he had going on? My husband didn't appreciate the change.

My first trip to John of God had been just about the last straw of his struggle to accept this weird spiritual stuff. In his mind, I had lost mine and was now a "Jesus freak." I remember a few days before I left again, listening to him all amped up about this great project he was doing. I vaguely remembered something about getting tons of money but it didn't seem karmically correct. I'm sorry to say I would, in the past, have been right there along with him in his excitement. "Wow, that's great, honey. Really. Wow!" I hear myself say, as an entirely different voice was playing in my head: *This is such negative energy. I need to leave this situation.* Things had come to a climax the night before I left on this second trip to Brazil. We had gotten into a very heated discussion that ended with him passing me a business card. "You'll need this lady's number when you get back," he announced. "Who's this?" I asked, but it was clear from the title under the name, "Family Law Attorney."

"You're divorcing me?" I said, a little shocked, yet part of me not surprised at all. Nevertheless, we smoothed things over that night. The business card was reduced to him saying that he was thinking about it but of course wouldn't go through with it. He suggested that we should seriously work together on patching up our differences upon my return. My sole goal that night was to make things as palatable as possible, rather than face the consequences of my clothes out on the lawn when I returned home. So as I left, on the surface, we had made up. Underneath, I knew it was over. I needed to figure out ways to minimize the impact of what I knew was going to be a very difficult, if not nasty divorce.

On the long flight to Brazil, my head was full of thoughts of marital issues and what looked to be my impending divorce. I wondered if the spirits could help me get through this one without too much pain. I begged and prayed for help. Then, could they please find me a nice guy for once!

As I sat with Josef that day, I was still married. Little did I know that back in Los Angeles, on that very day, at that very moment, my husband was sitting with his attorney drawing up the divorce papers. That little detail I wouldn't know for quite a while.

So, was I attracted to this man because I knew my marriage was over? I hadn't so much as looked at another guy the entire nine years. Even though I had been unhappy for some time, I never noticed anyone else, almost as if that emotion had been completely turned off. I'd occupied myself with other pursuits. Okay, I suppose I had looked at a guy, but even that only started during my first trip to Brazil. The spirits had in my healing, dusted off my Sacral Chakra, my relationship energy center, polished it up and given me a little tinge of emotion back. Now, today, it was rotating at full speed.

Was this my "nice guy" that I'd asked for? Already? Things do seem to happen quickly here. Could they have put me on "the fast track"? Whatever was going on here, it was fun, it was exciting, and I felt like I was a teenager again. I felt alive!

Josef says I look like the Angel Rita (St. Rita de Cascia) who appeared to João, marking the commencement of his miraculous healing powers. Boy, did he know the right thing to say! Josef would like to take photos of me to inspire his painting of this beautiful angelic being. There is a place at the top of the hill where you can see the entire valley, a wonderful place to take angelic pictures of me. I was flattered indeed to be his muse, even if this was just a pick-up line to get me to go on a picnic in the hills. It was certainly the most interesting and exciting pick-up I'd ever had. We make a date for a romantic afternoon over looking the Brazilian valley.

Collette, who'd accompanied me on the trip as a client but really as a friend, gets to be witness to our budding romance. She also happens to be an amateur astrologer, so later as we lounge in Frutti's Bar sipping on an acaí berry smoothie, Collette offers to check out our astrological compatibility on my laptop. I don't put much stock in it but, hey, it got me to Brazil.

"Your Sun lights up his house of spirituality and his Sun lights up yours. You'd make awesome partners in a spiritual project, and romance could feel spiritual in nature."

Interesting…. *"Could that be what I was feeling?"*

She continues, "Your Sun sextiles his Venus…." It's all foreign to me.

At that Spikey joins us, saying "Your what sextiles his penis?!"

He's got to hear this one! We feel like two teenagers caught gossiping about someone. But perhaps it's best left to fate. If the spirits really put us together, then I should trust their guidance.

CHAPTER 16

Interviewing in Brazil

A S PART OF OUR FILMING I interviewed different people about their healings and their experiences. There was one little girl that I very much wanted to interview. Her name is Anabelle. A "daughter of the Casa" who is probably John of God's closest right-hand, approached us. She told us that they would love for me to interview Anabelle.

It was a big privilege to be able to do that. I was the only person that had ever been allowed to interview her. And so I interviewed this beautiful sweet nine-year-old girl and her mom. Anabelle had been a perfectly normal little girl until she was about two or three years old and they discovered a cancerous tumor on her spine. After treatment, she was left paralyzed, with no feeling in her legs and no chance of ever walking again. It was a heart-wrenching diagnosis, but Anabelle's mother did not give up and when she heard about John of God visiting New York, she knew she had to go. After a profound experience in New York, Anabelle and her mom started coming to the Casa in Brazil. This was now her tenth visit.

The doctors said she would never walk again, that there was absolutely no chance. But each time she visited, she'd get a little bit closer, a little bit better. When I interviewed her, she was actually managing to pull herself up and walk a few steps holding onto the bars. She was getting her crutches on this trip and would be leaving her wheelchair. This was miraculous by all medical accounts. I asked Anabelle about the "surgeries" she'd had. She said that she'd been having invisible surgeries because John of God doesn't do physical surgeries on anyone under eighteen.

She talked about how much she loved coming here. I asked her, "How do people relate to it at school, and do they know about what you do?" I knew that it had to be difficult for her to explain her trips to her friends and teachers.

"I say it in a different way. I say I'm gonna go visit family, Uncle John and Aunt Heather," she responded with her complete innocence. Little Anabelle also talked about the angels and fairies she knew were around her during the spiritual surgeries.

Her mother talked with heart-felt emotion about the guides, and the volunteers who had invited them in like family. She talked lovingly about Heather, Medium João, the Casa mediums, and the volunteers who were so supportive and sent so much love. It was clear that the difficulty bestowed on her through her daughter's affliction had also brought gifts of joy. Both were receiving far more than a physical healing. She is absolutely convinced that her daughter is getting better due to her visits in front of the Entities, and she is sure that one day her daughter will be walking completely normally. It was such an uplifting story and wonderful opportunity to be able to interview Anabelle and her mother.

Another person that I interviewed was Dr. Zsolt, who has an amazing story. He was a medical doctor in Austria for many years, specializing in cancer patients. Ironically, he developed cancer himself. His bowel cancer had progressed aggressively, and after eleven surgeries and at stage-four, he of all people knew that modern medicine could offer no more help. He did not have much longer to live. His wife was very spiritual but the doctor didn't want to hear about natural healing. In his mind, his medical colleagues offered him the best medicine out there. One quiet evening at home, he caught a brief glimpse of a TV show, a documentary about John of God. He felt the energy of John of God coming right through the television. To his wife's great surprise, he turned to her and said, "We're going to Brazil."

Dr. Zsolt talks about his initial opinion of spiritual healing in the interview, saying, "Yeah, I didn't really believe in this. You know, I wasn't completely against it, but I didn't really put much faith in it." Then it's humorous to cut to my interview of his wife, separately saying, "He told me, 'Honey, I've been a doctor for over twenty years, and what you're talking about, spiritual stuff, is a bunch of rubbish.' "

Still, they took the trip to Brazil. I think it took several trips, but he was cured. He is now completely cancer-free and healthy. His medical tests confirm this. Now his role of "doctor" has changed dramatically. He coaches people with cancer on natural healing, and he brings people to John of God. I asked him, "Do all the people that come with you get cured?"

He told me that around ninety percent of them get cured, but not everybody. He then gave an example of one of his clients: "You know, I'm having a hard time because he says he wants to be cured, but he's more interested in going out to the coffee bars and socializing. I can't get him to take it seriously. I can't get him to sit in the current room and meditate, and that's part of the healing. You have to put in the work. If they prescribe you the crystal bed or prescribe herbs and then you don't take them, there's not a whole lot that they can do."

I had heard that from others. For example, one person told me that when he went in front of the Entity, he was asked, "Why are you not taking your herbs? Why did you not do this as I told you to do?" He was blown away that they knew. I think he did take his herbs after that!

Another lady I interviewed said she had asked the Entity if she could break the forty-day-no-sex rule. The Entity said yes. (Of course that would be the answer since we have free will, but this doesn't mitigate the consequences.) She said it was a bad idea, the sex was bad, and afterwards she said she was itching.

As she scratched her arm to demonstrate, I said "On your arm?!"

"No!" she said, "further down!" I knew then not to go breaking any rules.

As a medical doctor visiting the Casa often, Dr. Zsolt had earned himself a position close to John of God. He was often invited on stage to narrate the physical surgeries and assists regularly in the "infirmary" where people recover from physical surgeries. He has seen many miraculous events at the Casa.

As I discussed the physical surgeries and asked his opinion from a medical point of view, he told a particularly intriguing story. Once at the end of a physical surgery, as John of God was about to close the incision, he decided to hand the surgical needle to Dr. Zsolt who was observing and asked him to do the stitches. However, when Dr. Zsolt attempted to sew the skin, he found the skin was rock-hard and cold as ice. The skin felt frozen, and when he attempted to stitch, the needle just broke off. John of God simply smiled knowingly, and when he picked up the needle it went in easily and he finished stitching the patient. To the Entity, the skin was penetrable, but to the physical-world doctor it was impenetrable. It is apparently the energy of the spirits and the spiritual anesthetic that make the skin act this way. This is also the reason there is sometimes no blood or very little and why a person may barely have a scar the next day. The more one learns, the stranger this all becomes.

One of the strangest stories is that of Dr. Rogers. Dr. Rogers worked at a hospital in Brazil. He didn't believe in Medium João or any other healer, but his wife and daughter did and they sometimes visited John of God. Dr. Rogers had accompanied them to the Casa and was friendly to the staff, but he didn't believe himself. But then, as a result of his not so healthy lifestyle, the doctor developed some heart problems. His wife suggested that he go in front of the Entity but he laughed and told her that Spiritism was a bunch of rubbish. He was a medical doctor and believed only medical intervention could help. Shortly after he suffered a heart attack and was rushed to hospital. Unfortunately it was too late and he died on the operating table. His death was certified by three different doctors.

His wife was distraught and called the Casa seeking help. The phone was taken to the Entity. The Entity instructed the wife that she should stay by the body until 3 PM. The time of death had been

10:15 AM. It would be unheard of to leave a body for so long but since the doctor worked at the hospital, his colleagues thought there wasn't any harm in fulfilling the wishes of his wife. So a nurse was stationed in the room to watch over the body. At exactly 3 PM the doctor sat up, opened his eyes, and asked for a glass of water. The nurse ran out of the room in shock. Dr. Rogers recalls that during the time he was "clinically dead" he had vivid visions of talking with Dom Inácio. Today he comes to the Casa to share his testimony of a man who was brought back to life–literally! Of course, he is now a believer and travels around the country, sharing his story and praising the work of John of God.

Another curious healing was a man who was a professor at a prominent university in the States. He suffered from epileptic seizures that had become so severe that he couldn't work. He couldn't do much of anything anymore and was essentially an invalid, never knowing when these terrible seizures would occur. Somehow he found his way to John of God, where the Entities told him that his healing would take some time. Of course he was willing to take the time—anything to be cured. He was thinking a few weeks. A few weeks turned into a few months and then he was actually told by the Entity that he, in fact, would have to stay seven years!

At first it seemed crazy, but while he was in the energy of the Casa, the vortex of the town, he would feel completely healthy, normal, and seizure-free. The moment he would leave the vortex, he would start to feel sick and he would go into seizure. Literally, if he crossed the road at the edge of town, he would immediately have a seizure. It took a long time until he was told that he could leave for short periods, and I think it was about two years before he could leave for a long enough time to visit home. But he said that after he'd been gone a few days, he would feel worse and worse and couldn't wait to get back to Abadiânia. Eventually his health returned and he could leave permanently and remain healthy, but it did take those seven years.

He didn't waste his time during those seven years. He made his living as a guide and was an amazing one at that, performing a wonderful service for many people who visited the Casa. If I learned anything about the spirits, it is that you never know how they will work. They work in strange ways. Even the physical surgeries often make no sense to us—for example, "The Thing-Up-the-Nose Surgery" to fix a bum knee, or an eye-scraping surgery to cure a blood disease.

I am reminded of one of Josef's strange stories about his first day at the Casa. As they left the Casa to walk back to their pousada, Josef's eyes suddenly started burning. As they continued to walk, it got worse and worse. He looked to the others. "You must feel this. Are no one else's eyes burning? It must be smoke or something in the air. My eyes are stinging like crazy." Everybody else tells him that they don't feel anything.

When they reached the hotel, his eyes were burning so badly that he couldn't open them. As he cried for help, one of the Casa guides came in. Josef said, "I don't know what happened, but my eyes are so bad, I can't even open them." The guide asked him if he needed his eyes for work.

Josef replied incredulously, "Are you kidding me? Of course I need my eyes to work. I'm an artist."

The Casa guide suggested that perhaps the spirits were making him see, that they were connecting and showing him, through this experience, to pay attention. Then taking a cotton ball, she soaked it in blessed water and told him to place it on his eyes. Instantly, his eyes returned to normal. Such strange, odd ways the spirits work to get our attention. And this was Josef's first day at the Casa!

Entrance to the Casa de Dom Inácio

Bust of Dom Inácio in the Casa garden

The beautiful view from the Casa

Overlooking the lush green valley

Relaxing next to a crystal arrangement

Quartz crystals from the Casa hold powerful energy

Chatting with Medium João

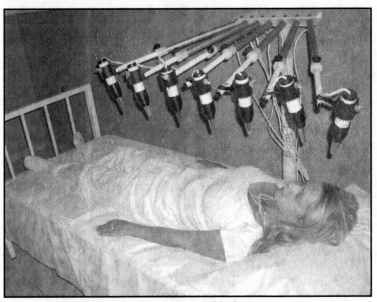

Gail enjoying a crystal bed session

Radiating energy after seeing John of God

Waiting in the Great Hall

Praying at the triangle

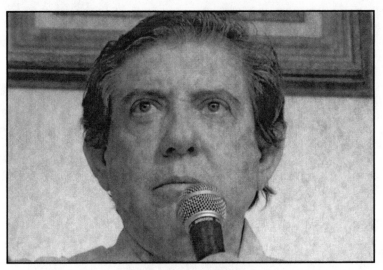

John of God in Entity

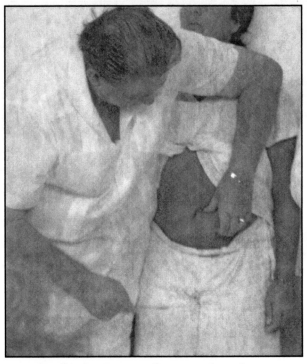

John of God in Entity performing a physical surgery

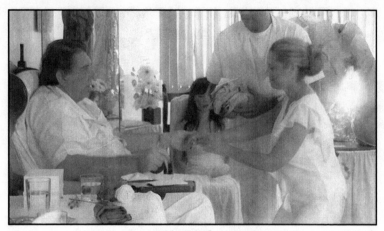

Receiving a blessing from the Entity

Dom Inácio, Jesus, and Mary

King Solomon

"HEALING PICTURES"
by Josef Schöffmann

Dr. Augusto

*Rivadávia Licinio de Miranda was an attorney general in life
and now is a spirit for the justice of God*

Looking for messages in the clouds

Life in Abadiânia

Gail leading a "Spiritual Journeys" meditation

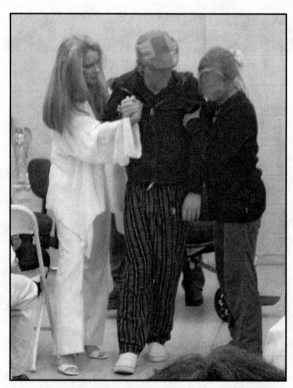

Gail doing a healing demonstration

Gail speaking at the Conscious Life Expo

Gail, Josef, and Harry filming the Brazilian landscape

CHAPTER 17

Getting to Know Medium João

THIS BEAUTIFUL SWEET MAN, João Teixeira de Faria, has dedicated his life to this great healing work and his missionary service. In loving passion for his calling, he takes all people without prejudice and gladly serves them. Millions have come on a pilgrimage to his center and have been received by his open arms. He presides over the sessions at the Casa twice a day, three days a week, and literally gives his body for the work of the spirits. I have heard from others that this type of full-body incorporation is extremely taxing on the body and therefore it must take a physical toll on João. His service to others doesn't stop there. On the days that he is not at the Casa he travels to other parts of Brazil and performs healings on people who can't make the long trek to Abadiânia. He is in anguish over those in poverty and is active in his charitable efforts to help. On occasion, he'll travel out of the country to do special live appearances.

Medium João is not only in charge of the Casa and its many activities, he plays a big part in the rest of the town as well. The pousadas, the cafés, the shops are all part of the spiritual experience and work closely in conjunction with the Casa. It seems João treats them as part of the family. He supports them and he regularly checks in with everybody.

João also has his ranch and various other businesses, including his crystal mines. Many people are dependent on him for their livelihood. The operations of the Casa itself and the staff are all funded through João's other businesses, through donations, and through the sales of the crystals and gifts at the Casa bookstore.

João tells of his humble beginnings, born to a large family of little means. At eight-years old, João was visiting his brother in a small town. As he was walking down the street he told his mother they must do something, there is going to be a terrible storm. His mother told him that there was no sign of a storm and there was only one tiny cloud in the sky. However João became distraught and finally his mother agreed to tell the townspeople. Within hours a massive storm came out of nowhere and demolished forty homes. After that João's mother was a little afraid that he was different. She felt that it would be best to take him out of school and he should instead learn a trade as a tailor. João would never learn to read and write.

João traveled far trying to find work. His healing incorporation started happening when he was just sixteen, barely a young man. His first touch with the heavenly realms was near a river where João stopped to rest, tired and hungry. An angel appeared in the river and spoke to him. At first he just thought this was a beautiful lady talking to him. It turned out to be St. Rita de Cascia. She told João to go to the Spiritist Center of Christ the Redeemer. When he went there, they seemed to be expecting him. Shortly after arriving, he fainted. When he came to, there was a small crowd around him.

These people were telling how he'd done these amazing healings, but he didn't know what they were talking about. King Solomon had apparently incorporated into his body and healed the people of the town. João spent three months at the center studying mediumship and trying to understand his gifts.

After this João traveled from town to town, trying to find work as a tailor. He also continued to spontaneously heal people, each time with spirits incorporating into his body while João "slept" through the process. This was not without the suspicious eye of the authorities who, over the years, prosecuted him as a charlatan and arrested him for practicing medicine without a license. João was thrown in jail, and even beaten, on more than one occasion for his selfless healing of others. João did not have an easy life growing up and living with this "gift" didn't make things any easier, but Medium João talks about his life and purpose as a blessing and never a complaint.

João, the medium, the person, is quite different from John of God incorporated. João has his own personality, his own likes and dislikes, completely separate from the Entities that work through him. When John of God is in Entity, it is the personality of the spirit who has taken over his body. When João is not in Entity, João is a family man, a rancher, and a businessman. He is married to a lovely lady, Ana, and he has several children. He reportedly loves to relax on his ranch.

One of the things that João likes very much is western movies. I have a funny story. We're at the Casa shooting with Liz who has worked on many of Clint Eastwood's films. Apparently this fact had been mentioned to Heather, who works closely with João, but we're not really sure whether it was the Entities that were speaking in João's ear or, more likely, that she mentioned it to him. One day we're packing up equipment at the end of the day and João appears out of nowhere. He comes up behind us, puts his arm around Liz and me, and starts asking excitedly about western movies and Clint Eastwood. Of course, we were a little taken aback at this.

Heather was translating because he's speaking in Portuguese. He wants to know about how they do the fight scenes in the films and all about the stunt men, the western riding, and the horses. He's like a kid in a candy store talking about something that is his childhood fantasy. He's so excited about this, and he starts to tell us how we should come back to his ranch. He tells us that he has beautiful horses on his ranch and would love to take us riding one day. He would also love to show us the places he first did his healing work. We couldn't believe it. Here is the great John of God, chit-chatting excitedly with us. It was so much fun.

Then he tells somebody to go and bring several copies of his book that Heather wrote. João personally signs a copy for each of us. He saves one book until the end and carefully writes a special message, making sure his autograph is just perfect. It starts "To Clint Eastwood..." and João asks if Liz wouldn't mind taking this to Clint himself and letting Clint know that he is a big fan!

We were all very honored to share in this personal moment with João and to receive a signed copy of his book. We wanted to do something nice back for him. It took me a little bit of effort but I managed to obtain a movie poster for one of Clint Eastwood's films, the Portuguese version of *The Good, The Bad, and The Ugly*. Liz took it to Clint and he signed it, "To John of God..."

João happened to be due to arrive in Austria with Josef for a live appearance in Vienna. I Fed-Ex'd the signed poster to Vienna. When John of God arrived, for his first order of business he looked at Josef and knowingly said, "You have a present for me! Can I have it now?" Josef laughed and went straight to his car and brought him the poster. João was ecstatic. He gazed at it with huge bright eyes and a grin from ear to ear. He said to thank all of us for arranging this. Everyone João saw that trip was proudly shown the autographed poster that he had been given. This one you won't see hanging in the Casa. This one he has hanging in a cherished place at his home.

It is nice to see that Medium João has a very human side. It's hard to think about it, but João is a person with his own life, separate from being incorporated with Spirit. I heard a funny story from Michael, who would often go to João's ranch for dinner. Remember, Medium João is actually unconscious, asleep, when he performs the surgeries at the Casa. Michael told me that the first time he was invited, they were sitting around the dinner table in the kitchen with a video playing. They were watching the videos from the Casa that day. João was saying things like, "Wow, look at that. He's cutting that guy open and taking the tumor out. Wow, that's amazing!" This is the first time João is seeing what was happening in this video because he truly was watching somebody else in his body performing the surgery. Michael said João was in awe and almost squeamish watching the videos!

One day when I was at the Casa, Medium João's wife Ana came for the afternoon session. She very politely lined up at the back of the line and didn't take advantage or ask for any special treatment, but simply lined up to see the Entity. When she got to the front of the line and was in front of her husband, now incorporated, she asked of the Entity, please, I would like to spend more time with my husband. The Entity told her to sit down next to him and meditate.

So she sat in meditation next to João in Entity for the rest of the session. It was amusing and yet touching to see his wife going in front of the Entity to work with the spirits. Clearly she is devoted to the work of her husband and has to sacrifice much of her personal time as well.

João has always refused to charge for healings. He doesn't even acknowledge himself as a "healer," rather stating that it is not he who heals, but God who does the healing. To visit John of God at the Casa remains free for all. There is a small charge for herbs that are sometimes prescribed. The herbs come from a plant that grows by the sacred waterfall. It used to be given as a liquid but it is now more conveniently dried and packaged in capsules. Although the same herb is given to all, the energy of the prescription is individualized by the spirits and incorporated into that person's herbs.

When I asked about people who can't afford the herbs, I was told that the Casa always helps those in need, so everyone is provided for. As another funny story goes, one day João is visiting a small town in Brazil where he is performing healings. One of the residents tells them that these people are so poor they don't even have enough food and couldn't then afford the herbs. To which the Entity incorporated said that Medium João is taken care of and has enough. The Entity told them to please take João's gold watch and keep it for the townspeople. And so the Entity donated the wristwatch right off João's wrist. Later, when the Entity left and João was given back his physical body, he told people that he couldn't understand it. He'd lost his watch and couldn't find it anywhere! They did eventually tell him and João was happy that it at least went to a good cause.

CHAPTER 18

Relationships Change

JOSEF HAS NOW LEFT for home. He's a continent away from Brazil and from my home in Los Angeles. I wondered if anything would really come of our connection. I tried to avoid feeling that space, that part of me that had been so vibrant just a few days ago and now felt desolate and alone. I pondered whether I really had feelings of missing him. This wasn't possible from such a short time, was it? But I did have feelings and they were very real. Now I had to face the fact that I probably wouldn't ever see him again, and I didn't even want to go where those thoughts would lead me.

The mature side of me asked, "Surely wouldn't you rather have the cherished memories of a few wonderful days than never to have experienced them at all? And if that is true, then you can just enjoy what you had, and whatever the future brings is meant to be." The other part of me wasn't sure I agreed. It felt like I'd had this crazy fun late-night party and now it was the next morning and I was left alone to clean up the dirty dishes. The thing I needed to clean up was my marriage. I loathed even the thought of dealing with it. With some good film in the can, I was out of excuses. It was time. I needed to force myself to address what I had put off for years—my home life, my marriage—and for this I would need some serious help from the Entities.

"How should I word my question to John of God?" I asked the translator and now trusted friend. "I think I'm at the end of my marriage. Things are not going to be good. I am terribly scared of the break-up and how bad this could be, how nasty the divorce could get. I just know that there is not going to be an easy out." I shuddered at the thought.

I toiled along with the translator. How am I going to present this? I don't want to say anything that is not spiritually correct. I don't want to ask the spirits to give me specific things, some kind of advantage, if that's not spiritually correct to ask. Is it right to expect the spirits to side with me? Do I ask for an end to this marriage in a loving way? Yeah, right! That would be asking too much of even the Miracle Man! Do I ask for protection and support through the break-up? I don't think I even want to bother asking to fix the marriage because I know the answer to that question already.

The translator writes down only about six or seven words in Portuguese. I have no idea what they are. But I do know that whatever is supposed to be presented to John of God, will be. I take my piece of paper and also my thoughts, my concerns, and my worries. In my head, I'm asking for protection, love, and guidance. I present this to John of God in Entity, wishing for a miracle. The loving Entity takes the translated piece of paper, and with a non-judgmental look of love, doesn't even ponder it for a moment before saying, "Yes, we'll help. Go sit on the crystal bed."

I take my prescribed guidance, my consult with Spirit, and I lie under the soothing crystals. I am open and vulnerable, passing my fate up to the spirits. Tuning in to the gentle music almost immediately, I drift off in a strangely disorienting manner. I rotate, floating gently up and out of my body. I feel like I've actually left my body and am floating softly above, looking down upon myself. Yet I can still feel the emotions in my body.

I ask, "Can you give me guidance in my marriage?" Then, as if a television were switched on, a visual starts, like a video playing in my mind. It is very clear, as if I'm watching a movie. I see the parting of the great Red Sea. I float into the scene and gently over the water between the parted waves. Massive columns of water loom on either side of me, a metaphor that would most easily take form as the looming event, a parting of the ways. At the very end, far in the distance, a vision comes into focus. It's a face, a painting, a beautiful painting of Jesus. I recognize it as a "Healing Picture," one of Josef's creations of love. Is this about Jesus being there for me? Or is this about Josef being there for me at the end of the path? Or is it both?

Then another beautiful face, again in the form of a painting, gradually appears. This one I don't recognize. It looks like it might be Josef's work from the style, but it's not familiar.

I ask, "What painting is this?"

I am told, "This one has not been painted yet. This painting will come in the future."

I didn't know on that day, but later I asked the spirits who it is. I was given an answer, quite a profound one. But I don't want to reveal it yet, just in case I am to change the future and thus inadvertently prevent a beautiful painting from being created.

My thoughts of wondering whom this is a painting of are broken by a narrator who announces that a new scene is about to start. I am given a date, a year in history. I wouldn't have known the significance of that year until the movie commenced and a piece of Americana was played out before me. The movie continued, vibrant, colorful, and realistic. I knew the history well, but what had this to do with my marriage?

As I continued to the watch the scene, I asked the spirits, "What does this mean?"

I'm told, "You'll find out."

"Who is my husband in this scene?"

I'm told, "You'll find out."

"What does this all mean? Why are you showing me this?"

"You will not understand until two weeks. In two weeks, you'll understand."

I continued to ask, but nobody was listening or answering. I had been shown what I was going to be shown. I was to wait two weeks for my answer.

I wander out of the crystal bed in a kind of daze. I questioned any Americans I could find. Most seemed to have been absent from their high school history class that day, but I was able to confirm the date later on the internet. If the date was correct, then it couldn't have been my imagination playing tricks. Something spiritual had really shown me a vision.

Well, I could keep you in suspense for a couple of weeks like I was, or I could just tell you the rest of the story now. So we'll leave

Brazil for a moment as I tell you what happened.

When I arrived back from Brazil, my husband was actually being pretty pleasant. We both knew that we needed to sit down and talk. He was irritated that having come back from John of God, I was still wearing white from my "surgery" and talking about my experiences. He was now completely convinced I had become a "Jesus freak." Other than that, things seemed quite palatable.

I had my big speaking engagement at the Conscious Life Expo in a few days, so I was in no mood to sit down and talk about the uncomfortable details of breaking up. He had many business deals on his plate, so he was in no mood to sit down either. The two of us were like ships in the night. I went to the expo and by the time I returned, he was already on his way to another city. We talked on the phone. Things remained cordial.

Eventually the inevitable I was dreading came. The day we would be together in the same room. The day we would resolve or we would part. That day finally came. Would I be able to get through an awkward discussion or would I, once again, take the easy way out and gloss over the issues, agreeing to stay in the marriage longer?

After almost nine years, he left. He was finally gone. He was gone from my life completely. To protect the innocent and the not so innocent, I decided that it was best not to share the juicy details of his departure. But I'll tell you this, I was completely spiritually protected. It was meant to be. In one fell swoop, he was cut out of my life. As with miracle surgeries from the Casa, I felt little pain, only the feeling of a beautiful miraculous healing. A great cloud had passed and the sun shone bright that day. They were right. Change was needed. With my invisible team holding my hand, change wasn't quite as bad as I had feared.

It was several weeks before it dawned on me to compare the crystal bed vision to what had transpired between the two of us. It was so obviously perfect, so close, so revealing that I simply couldn't see the forest through the trees. I checked the calendar. It was two weeks to the day! I was convinced in every way that I had been given the ultimate spiritual protection on this difficult life transition.

So what happened with Josef? We continued to talk for what seemed an eternity from opposite sides of the world. Many months later we would rekindle our love in a place on Earth that they call "paradise"—though any place we met would have been termed paradise. It is here that we would really fall in love. So is he "The One"? I don't know. I don't know if I am supposed to know. But it is not the arriving that is important, it is the journey along the way. And I can tell you this; the journey is certainly one of love, passion, and excitement. And as the stars said, a deep spiritual connection. Did the Entities put us together and do they have plans for us? That I am sure of. What exactly, I have no idea!

CHAPTER 19

Eye Surgery

BACK IN ABADIÂNIA, my visit is coming to a close. I wake up on one of the last mornings to the familiar sound of the country rooster crowing outside my pousada window. With only a few sessions left before I go home, this is my last chance to ask for something in particular. As I'm lying in bed, I start thinking about the one thing that's missing. I'm here filming my Spiritual Journeys documentary to *experience* whatever is going on at each place. I am to get involved with each guru so that through me, the viewers can experience their own spiritual journey. I've come all this way to be with John of God. I have communicated with the spirits and I have seen a lot of things, but there is still one thing that I have not experienced. The one thing that I cannot relate to personally, and therefore cannot really express through my own eyes to my viewers, is the experience of having a physical surgery.

I lay there thinking, *"I wonder what it feels like to have a physical surgery?"* I've interviewed a lot of people who had a surgery and heard their experiences, but I haven't experienced one myself. I ask myself, *"If I am 'to bring light to the people,' am I seriously lacking if I don't experience all that is offered here?"*

Now, I know that you can't volunteer for a physical surgery.

You have to be assigned a surgery by the spirits, by the Entity, and only then do you have a choice to volunteer for a physical surgery as opposed to having an invisible spiritual surgery like most. But I can't help but think that there must be a way. As I lay in bed, I contemplated how to make this happen and if I would indeed be brave enough. I've tried some crazy things in my life, but where is my daring gene when I need it? I mused that I couldn't do "The Thing-Up-the-Nose Surgery." That would just scare the hell out of me. Cutting my abdomen open and removing fibroids wasn't very appealing either. Now the eye surgery, the eye scraping, that one didn't look so bad!

By now, I had interviewed several people who had undergone the eye scraping and everyone seemed to say the same thing. They report that it was strange and felt weird. They could see what was going on and could see the knife coming toward their eye, but they all said that they felt no actual pain. They said that there was some irritation or redness afterwards, but this didn't sound like that big of a deal to me.

I began seriously contemplating the eye scraping. To be honest, after seeing it done numerous times, I thought that it didn't seem so bad. I found that I was talking myself into it. "Actually, it could almost be slight of hand. I mean, perhaps he only touches the eye very gently and that's why it doesn't hurt that bad. If you are in kind of a meditative state, are really quiet, and you've got a good pain threshold, this was something you could probably tolerate. It probably looks way worse than it really is." So I told myself....

There were other obstacles to my plan, as well. Even if you are assigned a surgery and choose a physical one, you still can't choose what kind of physical surgery you are going to have. That's up to the Entity performing the surgery. So how do I arrange for the Entity to choose to perform an eye scraping? Then it hit me. Lately, my up-close vision had been getting worse and I now need reading glasses which drives me nuts. I would really like him to improve my eyesight, if that's possible. Would requesting this ensure the eye scraping?

I believed this to be my best strategy. I'll ask John of God if he can fix my eyesight and, if it's meant to be, the spirits will organize an eye scraping for me. In fact, it could have been the spirits themselves that were putting these thoughts into my head in the first place. Did the spirits wake me this morning with the urge to want an eye scraping? I do know one thing for certain, if I'm going to get a physical surgery, I want to make sure a camera crew is there to film it! After all, the whole point is to share this experience with my viewers. There's no way I'm going through this and not getting any footage. Liz is no longer here, but a cameraman working with Josef is. I'm sure he wouldn't mind filming it for me.

With my plan in place, I go in front of John of God. My translation paper reads, "Can you help me with my eyesight?" As soon as he sees the paper, he grins, like he is quite aware and absolutely knows what my real intention is. He says, "Yes, surgery!" I have now been assigned a surgery for the very next session this afternoon. I am thrilled to have received the answer I was hoping for. However, now I am starting to get slightly nervous. I hope I have done the right thing here.

Immediately, I jump into work-mode. I find Marcus, Josef's cameraman, and ask him to interview me and film the surgery. He's happy to be there to capture it all on film. I'm now ready. My film crew is set and I can now take a moment to relax and have lunch. During lunch, I meet Nick, a newcomer to our pousada. Coincidentally, Nick has been assigned a surgery too, I believe for back pain. He unexpectedly tells me that he'll volunteer with me for a physical surgery. I'm excited to have a partner in this adventure. Perhaps he'll get an eye scraping like I'm hoping for, although there is a chance the spirits could do something else to me. I'm really praying it's not going to be "The Thing-Up-the-Nose Surgery."

When we arrive at the Casa, Marcus is already there and prepped to do a pre-surgery interview with me. It's probably the liveliest interview he's done here since I'm not going in for anything serious or life threatening, like cancer. My intention is really just to see what it feels like. Since I have interviewed many people who've had physical surgeries and they all seem to say that they didn't feel any pain, I'm not really that worried. I end up doing a very light and fluffy interview. "Yeah I'm going for an eye surgery and I'm a little nervous about it, but I'm excited and interested to see what it feels like." I sounded like I was going for a makeover or a new hairdo. Marcus laughed and said this was the most upbeat interview he'd done. A post-surgery interview might be an interesting comparison.

I hear the familiar prayers beginning on the stage. The afternoon session has begun. The physical surgeries are first. Nick and I are taken to the current room and are told to sit and mediate. I feel honored. We are the only "patients" sitting here inside this sacred inner area. The only ones communing with the spirits, meditating about the surgeries we are going to have. I'm a little nervous but more excited and glad to have Nick for company.

One of the Casa staff comes in. He confirms that we have no heart conditions and asks a few other medical questions. There are a few specific conditions that preclude the Entities from doing a physical surgery. We are then placed standing in front of John of God's empty throne. We are all by ourselves, just Nick and me, in this current room, standing in front of this throne with our eyes closed, communing with the spirits. It's strangely quiet. Just the sounds of the fans, but we are not alone. There is a sense of thousands of angelic beings whose warmth and love fill every corner of the room. The air is thick with spiritual energy and beings of the highest order surrounding us. To have the entire attention of this spiritual court was alone worth the volunteering. I contemplated how special I felt to be experiencing this personal spiritual attention. What an incredible honor to receive a personal treatment from John of God himself. I thought this is one of those moments in life to be cherished forever.

I can feel that the work is already being done. I feel beautiful energies all around me, as if they are realigning my energy field. I have a knowing that what's about to go on with John of God on the stage is more for show; the real healing is taking place right now.

I ask to check in with my personal spirits. I ask to check in with my dad in spirit. I try visualizing like I normally do but I can't visualize his face. I'm almost panicked. I can't visualize his face. I try to see my dad in my mind's eye, but I can't see him. I can't see that smile. He's not there. He is not connected. I try some of my other loved ones. I can't connect with any of my personal guides or my loved ones! Then Spirit lets me know that family members and other "normal" spirits have to stay back. They are there and they love me but they are yielding in awe to spiritual powers much bigger. I am under the care of the highest spiritual doctors and master guides performing miraculous healings. I'm here for surgery, and the doctors are in the house. Family members have to sit in the waiting room.

I felt these beautiful energies scanning me, aligning me, and performing whatever energy work needed to be done. In real-world time we were maybe there for a half-hour, standing in front of this empty chair. However, it was not time spent simply waiting around. I could feel that I was already being prepped for surgery. Or was the actual surgery being performed right then and there? The energy coming off the Entity's chair was sacred, beautiful, comforting, and loving. It had a warm, soft, pulsating rhythm like a train rocking you to sleep.

The next thing I feel is a draping sensation, as if somebody had actually taken a bed sheet, placed it over me, and pulled it around me. My eyes are closed and I don't dare peek. Then somebody grabs my hand and holds it. That somebody is John of God in Entity. His hand feels like a massive bear-hand, holding my delicate little hand. His energy is so big that I feel as if I am standing with a huge man, much larger than Medium João, the man. His energy spreads out from his body, making him appear like a 400-pound giant. It's a beautiful loving energy. What felt like a real sheet I now believe was John of God placing a spiritual sheet of energy around me, a spiritual veil to put me in a state of trance or subdued energy.

John of God takes my hand on the one side and Nick's hand on the other as he leads us slowly through the chapel-like current room. It is like being front and center of a very sacred, very special procession. Only our three physical bodies are present, but many spiritual bodies are surrounding us with love. This procession leads through the doors to the waiting crowd of onlookers and onto the stage. Walking with this beautiful Entity in John of God, I feel somewhat in a trance, somewhat subdued; floating slightly, yet still physically there, still physically aware of everything.

I feel the spirit energies all around me, protecting me. John of God walks the two of us up onto the stage. Probably five hundred people await, gathered around excitedly. I can see an array of cameras and lights pointing at us. As I am led up the ramp to the stage, I feel like I am floating up into another world. Present physically but not quite mentally.

The Entity places us individually and firmly against the wall. His assistants bring forward a chair and I am directed to sit. I move slowly, with assistance on either side, as if I am there but not there. I am to go first.

John of God stands behind me, cradling my head and brushing the hair gently out of my face, such a smooth, comforting feeling. I am so honored to be here, to be worked on, because I am being loved by these energies. I have been chosen for this very special treatment. He places one hand behind my head and then leans my head back gently. He opens one eye, my left eye, very wide. Even thought I feel in a trance, I can see all the people in the room. I see the cameras with their bright lights pointing at me. I see everything.

I next see the hand of John of God, holding the blade of what appears to be a kitchen knife, coming toward my eye. I reassure myself, *"Don't panic, people told you it feels weird."* But this is even stranger than I had expected. I can see this knife coming into my eye and moving across it, but I can't feel anything. It is certainly weird and uncomfortable, but I tell myself not to worry.

Then he came back for another pass with the knife. This time I was not expecting what was to happen. As he ran the blade over my eye, it was like shards of glass scraping. *"This is unbearable!"* I thought. John of God held my eyeball open with one hand as he scraped. I felt every little movement. It felt as if his knife were scraping a deep grove across my eyeball, like he had a piece of glass and was deliberately digging it into my eye!

I wince under the pain and tighten up. I can feel my eye watering. I'm trying to be a good subject. I'm trying my best not to move, but how can people do this and not move! Everyone else I've seen, they don't flinch. Do their eyes not water? Do they not feel this? I couldn't stop my eyes from watering. I could feel every bit of this "surgery." As he comes back for another pass, I thought again, *"Ooooouch!"* I feel my whole body tense up as he scrapes deeper. At this point I'm pleading in my head, *"Spirit, spirits! Where is my spiritual anesthetic?!"* I'm getting upset with the spirits. Why am I feeling this? Nobody else feels this—where is my spiritual anesthetic?!!!

In shock, my thoughts are filled with *"I cannot believe I'm doing this! What is going on here? I can feel everything! What has gone wrong?"* I see the knife approaching my eye once again. I'm now almost at the point that I can no longer stand it. I feel the knife dragging, yet again, across my eyeball. I am about to stand up, push John of God away, and say, "No more!" I'm absolutely done. In my mind I'm yelling, *"Spirits where is my anesthetic!"*

Right at my breaking point, when the surgery is almost complete, I get the message "Okay, it's time." Finally I feel the anesthetic. It was as if someone injected me with a powerful narcotic. A spiritual drug quickly flowed through my body. I had been through real surgeries in my life and it felt the same. My whole body went limp, yet I wasn't asleep. I felt completely subdued, completely relaxed. I could see the knife on my eyeball, moving back and forth, but now there was no pain whatsoever. No fear, no panic, no pain. I felt quite happy to be there and have whomever do whatever to me. I was in spiritual bliss. The whole visual of the room also changed. I was now in what looked like an old 1930s operating room with a large circular light above me. I could no longer see the crowds of people, although I knew they were still there. John of God passed the knife across my eye one last time.

John of God was now finished. He rubbed his finger around the rim of my eye, something that would have caused me to scream in agony just ten seconds ago, but now I calmly accepted. As he held my eyelid open, I could feel the breeze from the fan blowing directly against my eye—again, something that I presume I should not have been able to bear on a freshly scraped eyeball. I could feel this breeze and recognized that it was a cool breeze, so I had feeling, yet no pain, not even slight irritation. I was physically there in the room. I was physically feeling things in the room, yet I wasn't feeling any pain.

Why had I been allowed to feel that pain at first? The spirits were showing me the difference between spiritual anesthetic and no anesthetic, but why show me this difference? Well, hadn't I that very morning asked how it would *feel* to have a physical surgery? Did I not know the saying, "Be careful what you ask for?" After all I had seen and experienced, had I also been doubting the magic that happened here? Had I doubted that the eye scraping was real? In the back of my mind, I thought it didn't look that bad and that it would be easy to bear. Did I still not believe one hundred percent in the activities of the Casa? Well, today I had been shown. There was a spiritual anesthetic and there truly was something supernatural happening here at the Casa.

For me this was a turning point. There was no longer any doubt in my mind whatsoever.

I was guided into a wheelchair to be taken into the recovery room. As I left the stage, I was floating with beautiful feelings of subdued loving energy. I could still feel the wonderful relaxed fluffiness in my body. But all too soon, I felt the spiritual drug slowly disappearing. As I was wheeled into the recovery room, the anesthetic was dissolving away. The volunteers took off my shoes and lay me into bed, just as if I were in a real hospital. After about five minutes, the feeling in my body was almost completely back. It was as if I had just come around from a regular surgery back home.

Meanwhile, Nick was now the subject on stage. I didn't get to see it but learned later that they gave him "The Thing-Up-the-Nose Surgery."

CHAPTER 20

Fight Between Good and Evil

MY SPIRITUAL ANESTHETIC had almost completely worn off and I felt the pain in my eye returning. I could not open either of my eyes. Even my right eye was clenched shut because whenever I tried to open it, my left eye would hurt too much. I held my hands over my eyes in pain. I usually have a high pain tolerance, but I wanted to cry like a baby.

At the same time I was upset. What happened? I can't believe this! I felt a little in shock. I asked the doctors, the real medical doctors and volunteers present in the recovery room, if this was normal. Did people really feel like this? They seemed surprised at how much pain I was in and tried to calm me. I'm questioning everything. What did I do? Why was I not given the anesthetic until the very end? Why am I in pain now? I squirmed in my bed. I felt like I had just come around from a real surgery and the nurses hadn't yet arrived with my painkillers.

The only thing that gave me any respite from my anguish was to hear Nick in the bed next to mine going, "Ow... ow!" From his muffled voice, I imagined that he was holding his hand over his face as well as he repeated the words, "It really hurt. I felt everything!" At least I wasn't alone. I thought it was lucky that Marcus hadn't come for a post-op interview, as it would have been two invalids, each holding their face, moaning and cursing. In my head and perhaps out loud, I'm saying, *"I'm not coming back to this place. I can't believe I was so stupid. And I just volunteered for that! I think I've blinded myself!"*

I was blaming myself. I felt that I had just undergone major surgery for no real reason. I willingly asked for my eye to be scraped with a knife! I was in pain, upset, and totally confused. A medical doctor who believed strongly in the energy and the spiritual healers of the Casa tried to comfort me. The volunteers tried to tell me to relax and that this must be a part of my healing. They prayed and asked the Entities to relieve our pain. Nick and I lay there through the entire rest of the session, probably three or four hours. Still it wasn't long enough to recover. I worried about getting to my pousada and dreaded moving. I couldn't see a thing and cringed at the thought of facing the bright sunlight outside.

I felt completely helpless. I could hear Nick reflecting my feelings of pain and confusion. Then it was time to leave. I felt somebody putting my shoes on for me. It was Spikey. He helped me to stand and then, with me clinging to him, he escorted me out. Nick was holding on to Spikey's other arm. At least he could see, I thought. I could not even open my good eye. We stumbled out of there and into the taxi. Nick and I shared the backseat as we complained to each other about our pain. Our pousada was less than a block away but this taxi was an absolute necessity. I had to be literally carried from the taxi into my room. This was a new feeling for me to be completely helpless.

Nick and I crawled into my room and lay on my bed, side by side, two helpless invalids. "Why didn't we get the spiritual anesthetic?"

Nick was asking the same question. "I felt everything—did you?" He told me, "I felt this thing go up my nose. I didn't move, I didn't flinch, I felt like I *couldn't* move, but I felt it and heard it." Nick described how this thing went up in his nose and then John of God pushed it in further, twisted it around, and pulled a lump of flesh out. He heard one lady in the crowd gasp in alarm. That frightened him more than anything.

Despite our pain, Nick and I did see the amusing side of this whole scene—two invalids, lying side by side in pain who had willingly volunteered! We made jokes together. Did we get some spirit doctor-in-training today? Did they forget the spirit anesthesiologist? Did Spikey remember to put my donation in the donation box? Spikey assured me he had! He also told me that our spirit doctor had been Dr. José Valdivino, a very experienced spirit.

After a few minutes, Nick's pain started to wear off and a moment later it was completely gone. No swelling, no blood, no pain! Nick was feeling his nose in disbelief. He was a nurse and had been in nursing for twenty years, so he knew how impossible this should be. He knew that the physical impact done to his nose would normally cause massive swelling that would take weeks to heal. Yet in just a matter of minutes, all the swelling and pain had completely gone. Nick sat there, in wonderment. I, on the other hand, was still in pain and could not open either eye. I wasn't so thrilled for him.

I had pads of cotton soaked in blessed water covering my eyes and then eyeshades on top of that. Not only was my left eye throbbing, the whole left side of my face was in pain. My cheekbone and my left jaw were particularly painful. This was strange to me since John of God had not even touched these areas. My jaw actually felt the worst of all, like I had just had my wisdom teeth removed. But my jaw hadn't been touched! Was this pain all in my imagination? There was apparently no swelling or redness to account for it. Yet the entire left side of my face felt like it was throbbing.

I lay there for hours completely helpless, now understanding what it felt like to be dependent on the kindness of these human beings around me. Thank goodness for Spikey, who would take care of me for many hours after that. He stayed with me through the night. I held his hand tightly, afraid for him to leave me, even for a second.

Nick only stayed a little bit longer. He was now fine. In fact, he was even feeling blissful. He had surrendered to his fear and on the other side was a most wonderful warm energy. He left my room floating on air, feeling wonderful.

I was having a harder time releasing the fear. The rest of the evening I was trying to talk myself down, working with Spikey, who continued to reassure me. He told me that there was a reason for this and to relax. The Entities are working with me. He prayed for both of us and asked for white light. We both asked for the angels to come in and heal me. I could sense the Entities all around me, healing me and doing their work. It would go in waves. I'd get a wave of relief, a loving energy and comfort, a knowing that good work is being done. "We are taking care of you and it will be over soon enough" is the message I got from the beautiful energies working on me.

Then it would flip, as if it were a fight between the positive and negative forces within me. I felt negative entities as if they were attached to the side of my face. I thought of the pain and then the negative thoughts would come: "I'm not bringing anybody down here to this place!" I swore. There were moments that felt so dark, I actually thought I felt reptilian energies watching me from the corners of the room. I felt that there was a deep dark entity clinging to the side of my face. My jaw was aching. Was it a dark energy attached to the side of my face, bringing me great pain? I would then reassure myself, as I knew that the spirits had placed a protective energy vortex over the whole town and that no matter what I was feeling or how scared my imagination made me, I was protected here.

Then a wave of beautiful loving energy would come. I'd relax into it. I would try my best to think into that wave, to go along with that flow, and to know that something was being released and to allow it. Something energetically is happening, some positive is coming from all this.

Spikey talked me through for hours and hours. He changed my eye patches and poured blessed water over my eyes. He made sure I ate and drank. I clung to him. I panicked at the thought of being alone. There was a fight taking place between good and evil, albeit in my head.

As I lay there, my mind wandered to an event six months earlier. It was my amateur attempt at a ghost clearing from a house in Los Angeles. This particular house had been plagued with strange haunting events, and I had decided to take it upon myself to clear it. After all, I'd seen other people do this. Surely I'd be able to. In the midst of my inept clearing attempt, I actually felt a negative entity jump onto the left side of my face and cling there. I wasn't sure it was completely real, but strange negative events happened over the following days. I had sought the help of some amazing healers I knew and had done plenty of healing work on myself. If there had been something attached to me, I thought surely all this healing work had removed it. But now I'm thinking could it, in fact, still be attached to me, on my face? Had this negative entity been attached to me somewhat unnoticed for months?

As I now lay there, I felt that something really nasty was being removed from my face. Was this just my negative energy, my own dark and deepest fears, or was it an actual negative entity that had jumped on me all those months ago? Was it possible that I had been living with something and not realized?!

Spikey comforted me all night long and into the morning, holding my hand and taking care of me. I would go back and forth between nightmares of negative energies, which brought physical pain and fear, and those of loving energies asking me to trust, surrender, and release that brought moments of relief. The night went back and forth between something beautiful and something dark. I went from thoughts of "I'm never coming back" to "Relax and allow the healing to take place." It was a battle between light and dark.

The morning rolled around with a little relief. I could now at least crack my right eye and let a sliver of light in. I still did not want to get out of bed nor take care of myself, though. Spikey went to the morning session to ask John of God why I was experiencing this and if anything further could be done for me.

Spikey told me that John of God said, "We are removing something very strong from the side of her face. With this, pain is normal."

I was shocked. I asked Spikey, "Really, you're not making this up? He really said there was something on the side of my face being removed? He really said that?" I wanted to make sure he was relaying the absolute truth, word for word. This was my confirmation.

With loving compassion, John of God invited me to come back to the Casa that morning to lie in the recovery room. This was very unusual. I was very grateful and I lay there during the whole four-hour session.

I was being taken care of by the nurses and the doctors, and also I felt the spiritual doctors attending to me. There was a nurse from the 1940s, Sheila, who wandered in to see how I was doing. She was a beautiful blonde European lady, a little bit like Marilyn Monroe. (Oooh there's going to be lots of guys rushing to Brazil for a surgery now!) Then she went to check on the people from the war. They had just had their leg blown off, or something much worse than I. Of course, this was all in the spiritual world. Was I dreaming, or was I visualizing? I'm not sure. But I did feel the beautiful energy. I could hear the singing. I could feel the meditation of the current. I could sense all the spirits working on me. I was close to John of God conducting the morning session, divided only by the wall of this recovery room.

I couldn't open my eye outside in the bright sunshine, but here in this darkened room with my hand covering my face, I could finally peek out. I was relieved that it seemed I might actually be able to see again and maybe even be able to take my flight home the next day.

As time went on, releasing this bad energy, the pain gradually lessened. I felt the negative energy disappearing along with the nastiness that had been sucked out of my face and had been causing the pain in my jaw. As that pain was released, that negative entity was released too. I could feel it dissipating as the hours passed. It was leaving me.

Was this the reason for my eye surgery? All the other "reasons" I had made up: being able to show my viewers, for the sake of the documentary, to help my eyesight and not need glasses. Was this in fact the real reason? As always, Spirit works in mysterious ways and always for our higher good.

But there was another reason. If there was any doubt that this eye surgery could have been simply a trick or sleight of hand, a gentle touch, or something that with meditation somebody could bear, these doubts were completely taken away. I must admit, initially I did have my doubts. But this day, the spirits showed me otherwise. They showed me what it feels like without anesthetic. Then they showed me what it feels like with the anesthetic. And it was so clear and obvious.

Now, finally, I had absolutely no doubt that something super-natural, something very spiritual, and something not from this world happened that day. Without that feeling of pain, I think there might always have been that element of doubt. Perhaps they knew that I would share this with the world, and that if I was going to share this message, there could be no doubt in me. They proved it.

After three days, my eyes were completely normal, as if the surgery had never happened. There was no sign that there had ever been an issue. No redness or swelling, nothing. Did it improve my eyesight? Not really, but then again, I am not sure that was the purpose. I think I received the real purpose.

Why did poor Nick have to go through that too? No one else I know has ever experienced pain, why Nick? I don't know. Perhaps it was because he was with me. Or perhaps it was his path, too. Nick was luckier than I. His pain was gone within a matter of hours, and he told me that the rest of his night was beautiful and profound. When I later followed up with him back home, Nick told me that that day changed his life. It was indeed a wonderful, supernatural shift. After all, he pointed out, he had received brain surgery that day!

I can say after talking to many, many people, I have not found another person who felt pain. Everyone I interviewed assured me they felt nothing. Still, I am not sure that I would be brave enough to ever do a physical surgery again, although I am so glad I did and I wouldn't change what I went through for the world. I was given a gift that day. Not only to remove something that needed to go, but to be given absolute proof of the healing energy of John of God and the Entities at the Casa. I left Brazil to return home with a profound sense of gratitude.

CHAPTER 21

Coming-Out Party

I HAD A FEELING that my experiences in Brazil would shift things for me—how could they not?—but I didn't realize just how much they would. Remember my mission, the one that I accepted in awe and gratitude? Well, the spirits seem to have known I would accept, even before I knew that they would offer. I'm learning to never be surprised by how things happen to magically align, often before the question is even asked.

Just before I left on my second trip to Brazil, I was contacted by the gentleman who runs the Conscious Life Expo in Los Angeles, asking if I'd be interested being a speaker at this event the following month. Of course I eagerly accepted. Normally I would do a lecture on Animal Communication or Mediumship. However, I explained that I was going back to Brazil to film John of God. I told him how passionate I was about the spirit connection that I had received there and how it seemed that somehow I was able to help others connect to this energy. We both thought it would be a great idea if I could edit some of the footage and do the talk about my trips.

The event was just a week after my return, so there wouldn't be much time to prepare, but I knew this was meant to be. Unfortunately, I was offered my speaking slot too late to be included in the printed expo brochure. Without any promotion, my audience for the lecture might be a bit small, but that was fine by me.

Somehow, it all came together in time. I had lots of wonderful stories to tell, some filmed footage to show, and I was ready to wing it. The footage and the stories were great, but they were my back-up. What I really hoped was that the spirits would join me, as they did at the talk after my first trip. I wanted people at the show to share the beautiful energy that others had been receiving, the energy that some had even received just through my email. I hoped that the energy would be as powerful as it had been on that special evening a few weeks before.

I have a dear friend of mine, Aedan MacDonnell, accompanying me to play angelic harp music and a wonderful crew of volunteers. My helpers run off to get the lecture room ready but they quickly return to report that although it's still an hour before the event, people are already lining up. I had been given an average-sized conference room which seemed like it would be fine since I wasn't in the expo brochure. However, as the line outside the room continues to grow, it is quickly apparent that we need a bigger room ASAP.

The event promoters are now pleading with the hotel staff to find a larger room. I send a private little message out to the spirits. I know they must be working on it and will not leave us out on a limb. I am sure they will secure us a better room soon. In the meantime, more and more chairs are being crammed into the small room.

A line is now winding down the hallway. Where are all these people coming from? How had they even heard about me? People are saying they don't know anything about my lecture but that they were just drawn to hear me. Others are saying they don't even know why they are here, that someone else told them to come.

Finally the expo staff comes back. There isn't another room in the hotel available right now. This one will have to do. I am sure there is going to be a last-minute change. I look to the spirits: *"Help us out here, provide a miracle. You brought all these people, I know you won't leave us hanging."* At this point the staff have squeezed in as many chairs as possible and are starting to let the line in. I can't believe it. How can the spirits do this? Why would they have people show up and not have room for them? Do they want me to get this word out or not? Why would they bless me to do this, bring the people, and then not give me a decent room? Are only some of the people allowed to receive this? I can't believe that. I don't understand. I'm actually starting to get a little upset with the spirits.

The event promoters are shocked. Why did all these people come to see Gail and how do they even know about it? A few members of the press have turned up to see what is causing such excitement. The people in line seem to be just as confused: "I had to come, I have to get in, I don't know why."

I negotiate through the crowd to get to the stage. As I'm standing at the front, there are people literally two feet away from me, sitting at my feet. The event staff tells us that we can't let anyone else in because if we do and the Fire Marshal comes, they'll get in trouble. I felt terrible because people stood there for forty-five minutes and perhaps a hundred people will now be turned away. I have no idea why the spirits are allowing this. The show organizer asks if I could do another lecture the following day to accommodate those who were turned away. It's announced to those still in line that they are very sorry about the situation, but people can come back tomorrow at the same time to hear me speak.

I go ahead and start my presentation. I show some footage and talk about my incredible visit with John of God and my experiences at the Casa. I talk about the love that you feel from John of God. My talk is well received. I get some sympathetic laughter as I share my vulnerable side. Any nervous jitters I had are melting away. I now ask people to go inward, to go inside their heart and get into that quiet zone. I guide them to that place where they can feel good, where they can feel love. It is that place where they can release their anxiety and bring in happiness. Where they can bring that feeling of love into their heart.

As I'm doing this, I'm asking the spirits from Brazil as well as any other benevolent spirits that want to work with me to come in and surround these people with love. I ask the spirits to help them to clear their auras, remove any negative energy around them, and to help raise their vibrational energy. I'm asking the spirits (as I continue talking to the people) to come close and help align them; to help connect them with this God Source energy.

While I speak, I'm feeling this love that is coming down—this now-familiar feeling, coming down through my crown and filling up my heart. I feel my heart growing stronger as this feeling of love gets more and more powerful. I can feel the emotional bliss that is taking over me. I see the effect this is having on the room. This is not just me feeling this, it is everybody in the room feeling this. I see people's loved ones in spirit coming around them, being close to them. Perhaps subconsciously, people could sense their loved ones too. I feel that people's auras are being cleansed and the negativity being removed. Each person is receiving a healing at the deepest level. Beautiful spirits are here, in this room, helping to connect the people to Divine Source. As the energy in the room rises even higher, I see a beautiful white light coming down to each and every person. I see it filling their hearts.

As I looked out into the audience, a strange vision came to me. It was almost as if somebody had dimmed the room lights. As the lights dimmed, I could see a little flame, a little spark in each person's heart, in the center of each person's chest. I could see this little light, like a faint flickering candle, and as the spirits removed the negative attachments, removed the negative psychic dust, these little flames became brighter and brighter and brighter. It's as if these are little soul lights, lighting up. I think just about everyone in the room is now feeling this energy. Many are even sobbing tears of joy. Even the ones that are not particularly sensitive or don't particularly believe can feel the energy. I see people holding their hearts. Even some of the men are crying. I feel great joy seeing so many people being touched.

Spirits and angels had descended on our little space and were helping people reconnect to their true Higher Self, the God Source energy. Great healing was taking place that night. The spirits were blessing people. We all felt it. I, too, had been blessed as much as anyone in the room. I was on a euphoric high, reveling in my own blissful connection. I knew when people left that night that they had been reconnected to Source and their lives would change forever.

After my talk, the press descended upon me. One reporter told me that this had been "the most spiritually moving event I have experienced in years." What an amazing compliment! Especially coming from someone who specializes in this field and has interviewed many great spiritual leaders. I knew it was important to be humble, though, and explain that this was not something I had channeled nor even orchestrated. I had simply been directed to be here and the spirits had really run the show tonight.

I am filled with joy and gratitude that the spirits joined us, blessing us with their beautiful energy and healing us. I now know with certainty that I am on my path, spreading this glorious energy to as many as I can. After all, the spirits arranged this wonderful coming-out party for me! Tomorrow night, however, is about to hold even more surprises.

CHAPTER 22

A Bigger Arena

THE NEXT NIGHT I'm all set to repeat my "Gail Thackray's Spiritual Journeys" event. There's an electrified buzz, even amongst those who work for the show. It's all hands on deck as the hotel staff and my crew are busily preparing the room. Once again, a huge line starts forming an hour before. I'm upstairs in my room getting ready, being updated on all the excitement from my crew. "It's incredible! A lot of people that came yesterday are coming back tonight and bringing more people. They are all talking about how amazing it was last night. The line's winding down two hallways now!" The panicked organizers decide to move us into the big ballroom! Now I'm feeling really important! Where are these people coming from? The whole expo didn't even look that busy today.

A friend accompanies me downstairs. As the elevator doors open, there is a crowd standing outside. I think they must be waiting in the hallway for some big event. I didn't realize that they were actually waiting for me! As I step out of the elevator, they surround me. Everyone is staring at me. Nobody is mobbing me or anything—they are keeping a respectful distance—but I feel like royalty. I notice that some of the event staff are standing between us to give me a protective space.

As I walk to the ballroom, the crowd follows, including a few cameras. My friend whispers in my ear, "I feel like I'm with some major celebrity here." I'm thinking, *"Wow, my head is going to get really big with all this attention."* I arrive at the ballroom and see the line for myself. Even the event promoters are wondering where all these people came from.

The hotel staff begins letting people in while they continue to set up. I take this opportunity to walk around and thank everybody for waiting so long. People are looking at me, hopeful that I will smile at them. Why am I getting all this attention? I'm just a normal person. I didn't really do anything yesterday. This is just the spirits. I'm just as blessed as you are.

Finally everybody managed to get in. I thanked everyone for waiting, and I apologized to all the ones who couldn't get in the night before. I invited those who did come last night to share what they experienced. One lady stood up and said, "I couldn't get in yesterday and I went home last night and I had these weird dreams. I dreamt about a triangle and images of people. I didn't know what it meant." She continued, "I've had back problems all my life and I woke up this morning completely pain-free for the first time. When I arrived tonight I saw your triangle on the wall and inside the triangle were images of those who I saw in my dream! I don't know what happened, but just standing outside the door yesterday, I somehow received some kind of major healing."

The next person stood up and said, "I also couldn't get in last night. I have had a hip problem for years and I had a hip replacement. They were going to do another surgery on me. I felt the energy come from your room as I was standing outside. I felt it! This morning, my hip feels fine for the first time in—I can't remember—many, many years!"

Another lady stood up. "I couldn't get in yesterday and I have been having all kinds of financial problems. This morning I got a new job offer with a big commission. It's just unbelievable, and I know it has something to do with your event yesterday, even though I couldn't get in."

Then people who attended yesterday's lecture stood up and told more amazing healing stories. However, the ones that received the most seemed to be those that couldn't even get in! The spirits still blessed these people with the energy. Did the spirits somehow make up for the fact that these people were turned away? It was as if the mere fact that they had wanted to be a part of last night, their intention to be there, enabled them to receive help from the spirits. They had been open to come, and they were touched with this beautiful blessed energy. It seemed like an instant, spontaneous realignment of their energy had occurred.

It reminded me of the email that I sent out after my first trip. The email wasn't supposed to be enlightening in and of itself. However, the spirits had taken the opportunity to work through this online connection. Whoever opened that email and wished to be, even for a fleeting moment, connected with that energy received their wish.

I opened my talk by sharing my experiences in Brazil and some other things I had learned about spirituality and communicating with spirit. I talked about John of God, his miraculous healings, and the incredible things I had personally felt in his energy. Then I asked everybody to once again quiet their physical body, open up their heart, and open up their Crown Chakra. I talked them into a state of bliss and happiness, asking them to reminisce about a beautiful time in their life. I simultaneously asked the spirits to come in and to work on everyone. I asked for any spirits from Brazil who wanted to join us, as well as any benevolent spirits who had touched my life and wanted to work with these beautiful souls. As I asked the spirits to come in, I knew I didn't need to ask; they were already there. I was just the facilitator. I was just a physical body to be there, but the spirits were running the show.

As this beautiful energy came in and around them, I could also feel that people were now in a state where they could more easily contact their loved ones in spirit. Sensing their loved ones already around them, I asked the audience to be open to contacting them. I also asked their loved ones to communicate with them. From their physical expression and body language, I could see that they were experiencing this bliss, this love, this communication.

I decided to take this opportunity to confirm for people that the loved ones they were thinking of, and maybe even had a sense of them being there, really were present. I picked out a few people and did some of my mediumship demonstration work, describing the loved one and passing on messages. I went around the room saying, "Your brother Joe is with you" or "The friend that you lost in a drowning accident is with you. He wants you to know that he's okay and sends love." I was guided to give confirmation to these individuals for them and also so that everybody else in the room could see what was happening, that this energy was real. The spirits were showing me that it was important to demonstrate this so that people could believe in what they were sensing and feeling. It reminded me of John of God and the purpose of his physical healing demonstrations being to help people believe. It is hard for people to trust what they are sensing without the physical confirmation. I know this all too well. If I could give an accurate demonstration of the spirit world, the other side, the supernatural, then people could believe in their own senses.

I asked the spirits to continue to work on people, helping them to open up and feel their own connection to Source. As the spirits worked on them, you could actually see people's energy lighting up. Once again as I looked out at the audience, I could see these little flames, like candle flames, in the center of each person's chest, shining beautifully back at me. At first they are little flickering sparks, but they gradually shine brighter and brighter. I was looking at this audience that was a sea of bright souls looking back at me. I imagined it was a little like being onstage at a John Lennon tribute concert and seeing a sea of people in the dark, each holding a light against their chest.

It was a most beautiful sight—all these little flames of love, sparkling back at me. I could see the people physically but they were almost translucent. I was there in the room seeing the audience reaction, seeing them moved, but somehow I could see deeper than that. I could see these bright candle-like flames shining bigger and bigger, more beautiful; a room full of candles. I realized at that moment just how beautiful we all are at a soul level. These were lights of pure unconditional love.

It was the spirits who were helping these people connect to Divine Source. I could see a band of energy like a streak of sunshine coming down from heaven to each person's crown, through their head, and into their Heart Chakra. It was this energy that was the brightness of these beautiful flames. The brighter the beam of light coming in, the more these flames lit up, brighter and brighter. It became obvious to me that the spirits were removing any dust or negative energy that was preventing the person from receiving this pure Source energy. It is the life force energy that runs in each and every one of us. As the spirits removed the negativity from the people, their channel to Divine Source became more and more open. Each person was connecting to their true essence, their true soul, their life purpose, their joy, their happiness, their love. Their true inner beauty was shining back at me. I was watching people literally connect to God.

As I watched these souls light up, I could feel the same thing happening to me. I knew that I had a bright light in me that was also shining, and each one of us was shining at the other. Somehow being in this large group was helping to raise this vibrational energy, so each person was helping another. I felt so blessed to be here and to somehow help to facilitate this reunion of each person's own connection with Divine Source, something that they were born with, something that they were meant to have.

I asked everyone to turn to their neighbor, hug them, and send each other that amazing love. It was obvious that this energy was extremely powerful and even more so when passed to another. I invited all who wanted to share the energy with me to come up and give me a hug. As they did, I felt the love energy passing back and forth between us. Somehow the spirits were running through my aura, using the energy field around me, and touching them as they hugged me.

As people came up, I was compelled to share with them messages from spirit. Messages from loved ones. Little reassurances. Things about their health. I didn't know what I was going to say, it just came out. Later people asked me to expand on what I'd said or told me how profound the message was. Mostly I couldn't remember what I had said. It was odd. I felt like I was completely there, I didn't feel like I was channeling or anything, and I thought I had remembered every detail but when I tried to recall, I couldn't remember much from the messages I had passed.

Each and every person that night was touched. Each and every person that night received a soul healing. I felt this euphoric high. Was this me living my life purpose? I couldn't have felt happier. I couldn't have felt more blessed, more in tune, more full of life. I was so grateful that I had been chosen for this purpose. It felt so right.

I heard people talking afterwards about how this was the most amazing energy that they had ever felt, and how they knew something very special had happened that night. When I later reflected on how I had been upset with the spirits for not giving me a big enough room that first night, I realized what their plan was. As always, Spirit had orchestrated it just perfectly. Now where were they going to take me next...?

CHAPTER 23

Don't Talk, Do It

THE CONSCIOUS LIFE EXPO was a miracle weekend for me. I felt that I was living my life's path, although I was still questioning whether this was simply a one-of-a-kind weekend or if it was something I could continue. This energy was not something I had any control over or could summon up at will. I knew that this was a very special energy I was working with. I knew that I needed to treat this with great care and respect and not in any way abuse this energy for my own gain. I was afraid I might lose this "gift" if I was not careful. I'd had a little taste of the limelight and must admit I loved it! I could see that these amazing circumstances could be easily abused for personal power and financial gain. Although I had no intention of doing that, I was still afraid I might do something inadvertently. Well, apparently the spirits had already tested me—twice.

What were the two tests? I didn't even know I was being tested at the time. The spirits reminded me of two things. The first was when the Expo organizer asked me if I wanted to do a lecture. He asked me how much I wanted to charge, telling me that speakers usually charge around $30 to $50 for admission. I told him, "I don't want to charge, it just doesn't feel right." I felt that if people wanted to buy crystals I brought back from Brazil or a CD, that is different. That is something tangible they have asked to purchase. But as far as just being here and receiving the energy, I don't feel like charging. I want to do that part for free. I'll admit that to charge money was tempting, but it did not feel like it was the right thing, right now. I felt that it was more important to get the word out now and I believed the spirits would provide for me in other ways.

The second test was during an event where I was introduced as a "great healer" with examples of my "miraculous healings." Then some other people stood up and testified to the amazing healings they received from me. However, as soon as I opened my talk, I was compelled to correct them all. I told everyone that I cannot take the recognition for these healings. Yes, people were experiencing amazing things, but that is a result of their own connection to Divine Source and to the spirits who helped them to connect. "It is not me," I insisted. "I'm just as blessed as you to be here. I am just as amazed and in awe as you are."

I had passed their tests. Still I asked for guidance to stay on the right track. I was afraid of my own human frailties.

As word got out, I started to travel to other cities. I was still doing events at my ranch, but I really wanted the energy of larger groups. Spiritual expos provided a forum where the energy could be shared and hundreds of people could expand together. The larger the group, the more energy generated, the stronger the connection. This was the collective coming together, truly as one, to receive the blessing as wholeness, the most powerful energy of all.

I next had the opportunity to speak at the New Living Expo

in San Francisco, a very large forum. My first talk went amazingly well. People were moved and the spirits gave us a powerful blessing. However, the hall was so big and the acoustics were so poor that people couldn't hear me unless I was shouting into the microphone. The sound techs at the back of the room didn't realize, and so I conducted my two-hour event by shouting. We had a wonderful event. Everybody loved the energy and many powerful healings took place. I was once again blessed to be a part of this.

However, as I left to the hotel, I knew I had strained my voice. Shouting for two hours had been hard, though it seemed like I was okay and my throat wasn't hurting. I went to bed early, but a couple of hours later I woke up. I went to the bathroom and I knew something was wrong with my throat. It wasn't hurting, it wasn't scratchy, but when I tried to talk, oh my! I couldn't speak a word. I had completely lost my voice!

"What am I going to do?!" I'm questioning the spirits, "If you want me to go on stage tomorrow, how am I going to do this without a voice?" I am completely and utterly speechless. One friend goes down to the bar and gets me whiskey and sugar. Another gets herbal remedies and some homeopathic stuff. Nothing is working but I am on the way to a hangover!

Obviously this is spiritual in some way. My throat doesn't hurt in the slightest, I just have no voice, but why? What are they testing? Am I not supposed to be doing this work? Did I upset the spirits? I'm asking the spirits over and over, "What am I to do?" I go back to bed pleading, "Please give me an indication of what I'm to do here."

Then message came back, "You need to stop talking so much. Don't talk, just do!"

Okay, well, how am I going to do that? I can't just stand up there and stare at people! Then I'm given the message to use the CD recording I had of my meditation. This recording of my meditation, accompanied by Aedan on the harp, was already producing miraculous results and people were reporting healings similar to ones received at my events. The message given to me was that I should play the CD and concentrate on just allowing the energy flow and work with people to connect them. "We want to show you how powerful your recorded work is and that we can travel through this space. We want to show that you don't need to talk so much," I'm told. Still, I think pushing me out cold turkey is a little harsh. Then I realize that in my previous events, I've been giving a whole lecture, talking about my experiences, adding in some amusing stories, and half the session is over before I get to where I actually help people to connect. Okay, spirits, point taken!

Unfortunately, my voice is still gone. At breakfast I can only muster a faint whisper. I've regrouped with my team and we're going over the options. Really, it's quite hysterical. We have to laugh about the situation—a speaker with no voice.

A couple of hours later, I'm up. A show announcer comes on stage and explains that I have completely lost my voice and that we are going to use a CD of my meditation. He asks everyone to listen to and connect with my recorded voice. Meanwhile, I am calling in the spirits and setting the energy.

The recorded meditation was powerful, and I could see the

energy flowing and the spirits working through the recording. I could see people opening up and their candle flames turning on. I then invited people up, hugged them, and worked with them in whatever way I was guided. I asked the spirits to help me connect to their energy field to allow the spirits to run their energy through me.

By the end of the night, I see the same beautiful glow of candle flames shining back at me. These beautiful bright souls, each and every one, was moved. Again, people felt the energy. People were receiving the healing, the blessing, the connection with Divine Source. Many people bought the CD to continue doing this meditation at home, and I knew that the spirits would continue to work on them through this medium. Strangely enough, right at the end of the night, I was able to talk just a little bit, just enough to give a short closing.

Within a couple of hours, my voice was completely back and I had learned that I didn't need to do so much of a show. It wasn't about talking so much. It was about feeling, doing, and bringing in that energy and helping people to connect. Very little explanation was needed. Talking about it was not the most important thing; allowing people to feel it was. And they would feel it. They would know it. I didn't have to explain it.

CHAPTER 24

My Path

WITH THE POWERFUL ENERGY that seemed to bless me after my visits to John of God, news of the increased energy at my "Spiritual Journeys" events got out. More and more people came to see me. Some people received the energy just by thinking about coming. Each event was a little different. I was being guided by the spirits, and they would surprise and amaze me. I remained in awe of the process.

Sometimes I feel guided to show proof to help people to set their mind into belief. I may do a short mediumship demonstration, giving messages to specific people from Spirit, such as "Your uncle is here, the one with the initial 'J' with the red car who was in the music biz." This is not only so that the individual feels the connection, but also so that others can see it as a demonstration of the existence of another world. This can help to confirm for them that their feelings are real, to have faith in those feelings, and that they can sense their loved ones in spirit. When the audience is in this spirit veil, their loved ones are close.

Often I will be given information about physical ailments of people in the audience, letting them know that Spirit knows and will be working on those specific issues. "They are working on your ankle, the one you had surgery on." "We are going to work on curing that stomach ulcer tonight." Etc.

When I pass on these "gems" from the spirit world, you can tell by the individual reactions that I have hit a chord. Their look of shock and awe inspires everyone else in the room. Of course, I can't do this for the whole room, but I give enough samples for people to trust that the spirits are there. It seems important that people can be open to this other world and therefore ready to receive the energy. This is perhaps the removal of our first layer of blocks.

This honestly is the part I most fear. It takes a tremendous amount of trust. I have no idea when I point at someone what I am about to say. Sometimes I open my mouth and say, "I am getting the message that…" yet I have no idea what is going to come next. It's a very strange feeling. I feel very vulnerable. I am always fearful that nothing is going to follow or what I say won't make sense. It is especially daunting in front of a large audience! This is the most difficult for me, trusting that the spirits will always be there. So far they haven't left me hanging.

The odd thing about these messages from Spirit is that I usually only have a vague recollection of what I have said. I think I will remember everything. I don't feel spaced out. I don't feel that I am "incorporated" with spirit, but when asked later, I often have no recollection of things that I said. So I put myself out there and trust that the spirits will guide me.

The spirits direct me in what is right for each group. Sometimes the spirits ask me to set the belief by demonstrating healings. I feel that every single person in the room receives the energy as well as the healing physically, mentally, and emotionally. However, sometimes it seems necessary to demonstrate the healing to help people to be more open to it. The first time I was asked to do healing demonstrations, the spirits told me to add in my Reiki. They wanted me to bring volunteers to the stage and to perform cutting cords, clearing auras, and psychic surgery.

Weren't the spirits already healing everyone in the group meditations? Yes, they were, but I was now to allow them to use my physical body to direct the energy to individuals as a demonstration. I had always known that Reiki energy was in fact Divine Source or God energy. It is the same energy that I had discovered in more places than one. Which makes sense since we all connect with Source differently because we all have different ideas and upbringings. Some people resonate with Theta Healing, some with an Indian guru in an ashram, others through prayer, some through meditation and yoga. However, I believe that all modalities lead to the same path and the energy itself is One–that is, God.

It is the beautiful warm loving energy I feel when I tune into the spirits on the other side. It is the same feeling that I sense when doing Reiki on people. It is the same energy that I felt from the Iveron Icon weeping myrrh oil. It is the energy I feel when animals "talk" to me. It is the same feeling I get when my daughter looks into my eyes and says, "Mommy, I love you." It is, in fact, God energy, and that is at the core of each and every one of us, and this is pure love.

In the first healing demonstration after my new connection, I invited some people on stage. A man hobbled up, bent over and walking with both the aid of a cane and his friend. It was a huge deal for him to even get to the stage, and he slumped down in a chair. I instinctively placed my hands on him. I cut cords, as I would in a Reiki session. Then the most amazing thing happened. Something came over me, I don't know what, but I threw his cane across the stage. I grabbed the back of his chair and demanded that he get up. He said he needed his cane. "No, you don't need that anymore," I said in a firm no-nonsense voice. Yet inside I'm thinking, *"What am I saying? I need to give him his cane back. He needs it."* The man pleaded for his cane. "If you want it, go get it yourself," I said in a very unfeeling voice, pointing to where it had landed at the other side of the stage. Again, it's as if I have a double personality and I'm arguing with myself. *"How could I be so unfeeling? He obviously needs his cane."* But then he stood up and to his amazement, he stood up straight. He had no pain, which was obviously a shock to him. He took a few cautious steps before realizing that he was able to walk, standing up straight and with no pain. He didn't need his cane. As he walked off, I was as surprised as anyone.

I had others that came in wheelchairs to whom I demanded, "Get up and walk." I didn't believe this was possible, yet this came out of my mouth. And to my surprise, they walked! I knew there was some other powerful force behind my words and that I was simply the physical presence.

Tremendous healings took place. Sometimes they were obvious, and sometimes I would find out much later. I brought a lady on stage who didn't have any apparent physical ailments, but I felt guided to cup my hands around her throat. I felt heat, like a furnace, coming from my hands. She didn't seem particularly moved and didn't offer an explanation or confirmation. I may not have ever known anything further, but she happened to attend another of my events about a month later and she took me aside. "You didn't know this but that night that I volunteered and you put your hands on my neck, I had stage-three throat cancer. After that night it was completely gone." She thanked me profusely and I told her, once again, it's not me, it is Source energy. This is your connection with Divine Source. This is the natural state of healthy being that you are supposed to experience. Give gratitude to the spirits that helped clear you to be accepting of this, but thank God for the healing itself.

I had been working with spirits before my trip to John of God but somehow since I came back, something more was happening. People were receiving a strong energy, an opening and a connection of their own, spontaneously, just by attending or even thinking about attending my events. Large groups were receiving a healing, instantly and spontaneously. I no longer had to "work" on a person. It was happening automatically and to many people at once. What truly struck me, though, was how most reported that it was not a one-time event or a one-time miracle cure—the energy had somehow continued to open up amazing, positive things in their lives. The spirits wanted to share this energy, and I was able to bring groups together to receive it. People received a soul healing and a direct connection to Source itself bringing new direction, more joy, better health, and more abundance. Their energy had been realigned. This was that person's individual connection with God and was theirs to take home, theirs forever. There was no need to return to me. I thought back to when I sat in the little chapel room in Brazil and God spoke to me. I asked to be able to pass this feeling to others. I had been blessed to be a part of this. To see this now happening was the most incredible blessing I could ask for. And this was all possible through this beautiful person, John of God.

My own journey began with mediumship, connecting with those on the other side, through Reiki and other healing arts, to assimilating knowledge from shamans and other traditions, and to a magical journey to Brazil where I met John of God and beautiful healing Entities. All of these helped shape me and direct me toward my path. All were special to me. I want to bring this to others as well. Helping people find that "special thing" that helps them to feel their own connection to Source has become my life purpose. Whether I will continue with this format, I don't know. What I do know is this feels right, this feels like my mission.

I know that I am following my true destiny, my true soul purpose.

CHAPTER 25

Revisiting John of God

A YEAR LATER I returned to Brazil. This time I came with Josef, not only as a sweet reminiscence of our meeting but also to blend our talents in film. We filmed the story of Medium João, his early life, and the emergence of a great spiritual healer. We traveled around Brazil searching for the house where João grew up, the river where he encountered St. Rita de Cascia, and the Spiritist center where his mediumship began. Over a beautiful two weeks we interviewed those who came to the Casa seeking spiritual help and heard many more stories of extraordinary healing. We followed my continuing journey and documented another miraculous visit to John of God. Many afternoons Josef and I sat on the hill overlooking the Casa waiting for the perfect sunset and enjoying our time together.

Although I experienced many miracles, paranormal experiences, and surprising serendipities, one is particularly worthy of note. Although both Josef and I had been given open blessings to film, each time we came we had to be once again approved. This week the Entities had not been receptive to filming, and we had been sent to sit in current on more than one occasion to earn the right to film. This particular day Josef and I were standing in line about to request filming permission from the Entity yet again. We were right outside the door waiting our turn to enter when I noticed a girl walk out of the current room. Nothing was unusual in this. She was a young girl and wore a white outfit as everyone did. Then I noticed something very strange; flames were coming out of her chest. For a second my mind tried to reason this oddity in my vision and find an ordinary explanation. Then when my mind couldn't compute what my eyes were seeing, the blood suddenly drained from my face. I felt a cold sweat on my body and I had to sit, lest I drop to the floor in a daze.

A strange energy field seemed to come over me. Josef was concerned and ran to my aid. It was now time to enter the current room. Assisted by Josef, I stood up and continued in line, but now I felt odd, not quite there. It was as if I were walking in front of myself, not quite in my body. There was a beautiful serene feeling that accompanied me, even though I felt somewhat unlike myself. I was glad Josef was by my side, half-waiting to catch me if I were to faint. As we came up in front of the Entity, I dropped to my knees and held his hand. There was a huge surge of energy that felt like it came through me and from my heart to his. I was completely overwhelmed by the energy.

John of God seemed surprised and smiled. He turned to the interpreter to give a long explanation. It was translated to us that he wasn't going to allow any filming today but he'd felt a huge, beautiful energy coming from my heart. He felt that it was from a soul level and, for this reason, he blessed us to film. He invited us to come back and film by his side.

Something had happened in the moments before I entered the room. I wasn't sure whether an angel or a spirit had swept me up and walked with me or, if my energy had been suddenly aligned by the spirits. I still don't know if the girl had been real and I had warped into another dimension to see the energy from her heart or whether she had, in fact, been a spirit. It had looked like a real girl. Whatever happened that day, I had felt a great and powerful blessing from Spirit and they had come with me to deliver the message to the Entity. Someone or some power was certainly helping me.

After I left this experience, I wandered in a daze around the gardens. I was floating on air not knowing quite where I was, in a cloud of blissful energy and emotionally moved to weeping. It was at least thirty minutes before I felt any sense of normalcy and could relay my experience without bursting into tears.

The following session we took up the invitation. Josef and his partner Harry filmed me as I approached John of God. This time I brought healing requests from people back home. Dr. Augusto was incorporated. As he wrote prescriptions for the distance healings, we chatted a little. I thanked Dr. Augusto for the help I had received on each of my previous visits that had certainly given me a miraculous outcome. He was interested in my life and asked what type of work I did. I explained that we were making a beautiful documentary to show the great healing here.

He looked deep into my eyes and said, "You have a great purpose."

Coming from such a great spirit, I was in awe of his words and felt great responsibility in his prediction.

"When can you come back?" he continued. "Can you come next week?"

"No, unfortunately I have to go home," I said. "But I can maybe come back in a month or two."

"Come back soon!" he said. "You need to come back at least one more time. Come back as soon as you can."

This request I will have no problem fulfilling! I was honored he had an active interest in my progression.

There were many more touching moments with the Entities. The experiences over the remainder of our stay were often profound. The spirits were just as clear and communicative as they had been previously and the sessions in current once again, connected me to the beautiful energy here.

One particular day the energy in the current room was very powerful. I was sitting in meditation while Harry was filming me. As Harry swept the camera across the room suddenly a large, white spot of light appeared on the lens. As the camera moved, so did the spot of light. It was vaguely opaque and misted the faces of the people meditating as the camera passed over them. Harry took out a cloth and tried to wipe the lens, but this orb of light remained. He tried again with cleaning solution, but still it remained. In fact, it seemed to morph shape slightly, which couldn't possibly be a spot on the lens. It also became darker as it passed over a white wall and lighter over a dark background, not something any moisture spot could do. After about thirty minutes the current session was finished, but the orb remained.

Harry reported to Josef that something had gone wrong with

the camera, and they may need to buy another one. Then, while the two stared at the screen, the orb got smaller and smaller until it was just a pinpoint, and then it disappeared. They realized that this was no camera error. It wasn't something on the lens. This had to be a spirit! Had we caught a video of a real spirit?! How blessed we were to be allowed to see this presence.

We had fantastic footage and had covered almost everything there was to report. All except one thing we truly wanted—an interview with the big boss, Medium João. Even with Josef's close relationship and the many powerful blessings I had received, it was hard to arrange for an interview with this very busy man. But on the very last day, at the very last moment, Josef came running out of João's office, ecstatic. "We have an interview! We have an interview! With João! Now!" I don't know what miracle Josef pulled off, but we quickly rushed our crew together and within moments, I was sitting side by side with the great Medium João.

He sat warmly holding my hand and talking emotionally about the healing work, the spirits, and most of all, his devotion to God. For probably thirty minutes he cried, he laughed, and he shared openly with us. He spoke of his difficult life growing up but without a moment of complaint. On the contrary, he expressed how blessed he felt to carry out God's work. He anguished about poverty and his personal devotion to preventing suffering. He also described the healing work itself. As he spoke the words, "through God all things are possible," I felt his love, his energy, and the truth of his soul. We were very blessed to receive so much of this man's precious time to share about his healing, his vision, and indeed his energy for our viewers.

When the interview was complete, he made sure no cameras were rolling. João turned to me and delivered a personal message. He expressed that I was going through certain spiritual "tests" and that to know I was being divinely guided and protected. He was absolutely correct and I realized then, that even when João is not incorporated and "asleep," João the medium is still very much connected to the other side. I thanked him for the wonderful insight. I was honored, the reassurance could not have come from a higher source than he. "I just felt I needed to tell you this," Medium João said.

Now I will leave you with one last story. As I mentioned, I brought several photographs of people who couldn't come to Brazil themselves but desperately wished for a healing with the Entities. One such lady, Lauren, was a gemstone vendor at one of my spiritual fairs. Two months earlier, Lauren had told me the sad news that she had cancer. She asked if I could take a photo of her to John of God. I told her I wasn't going for a couple of months, but I would gladly accept her photo right away and ask the spirits to start their work. Right before I left on my trip, Lauren dropped off an updated photo at my office. As I presented this photo to the Entities, I noticed that it stated on the back of the photo, "I had cancer but all cancer cells have been eradicated and I would like a blessing to remain healthy." When I returned I mentioned to my assistant that I must have misheard her the first time she gave me the photo. My assistant told me that when she dropped off the second photo, Lauren assured her that they had already cured her.

I called Lauren to find out her story. When I first spoke to Lauren, she was undergoing treatment for liver cancer. It was so severe and widespread that it was inoperable. She had been told that she had only a short time to live. I remembered that on the day I received her photo, I sat under my triangle and told the spirits that I would be visiting John of God in two months and would be bringing Lauren's photo, but could they please start to work on her now. A few days after this, she went to her doctor for her regular visit. The doctor was absolutely astounded. The cancer had completely encapsulated itself. This meant that they could now operate to remove it. Shortly afterward she underwent a successful surgery and the cancerous growth was removed. The doctors expected to see other cancer cells spread throughout her liver and other organs as before, but now they could find no trace. The operation had completely removed every cancer cell. The doctors said this was unheard of and that the cancer cells encapsulating spontaneously was not just a medical impossibility—it was a miracle!

I share this as an example that the energy and the healing work of John of God and the Casa is indeed miraculous and powerful. Just in the asking, Lauren received from thousands of miles away. Instantly and spontaneously.

I truly believe that the message, the healing, and the feeling can and will transmit across time and distance through film, audio, prayer, all ways of connecting—even through the written words on this page!

My wish is that this book has inspired you to listen to your inner voice, to listen to the spirits around you, and to know that you are surrounded by guides and angels who are just waiting for you to ask for their guidance. Don't ignore those little "signs." Yes, you do feel them and you do sense your loved ones. We are all mediums and the veil is becoming thinner and thinner.

If it is a dream of yours to go to Abadiânia and to visit John of God, ask the spirits to find a way. They are listening and they will surely get you there.

Now I leave you with this: it is your God-given right to connect to this beautiful Source energy, to know it and to feel it. I ask with Divine love and protection for this powerful connection to be there for you, today and always. In reading this book you have already asked, you are already connected. Anything is possible. So live your life in health, love, and prosperity.

Medium João has devoted his life for almost fifty years to alleviate the plight of other human beings. He is not only a miraculous healer; he is a living phenomenon. I doubt that ever again in our lifetime will we have the opportunity to come face to face with a person so gifted. For those that can make the pilgrimage to Brazil, it will change your life forever.

Acknowledgments

People who visit John of God often remark how their healing began with the love and caring they feel from the staff and volunteers at the Casa, the pousadas, and the town of Abadiânia. That just being there they feel like they are part of a family. This is absolutely true. I received the love and open hearts that seem to be given to everyone that goes. I want to acknowledge those that dedicate their time to the work of the Casa and provide that nurturing cocoon through which I experienced this most miraculous journey. In particular I would like to express deep gratitude to Martin, Diego, Vinicius, Costas, Heather, Sean D., Dr. Zsolt, Nina and the staff and volunteers that helped me on my journey.

I would like to thank all those who openly shared their stories, those at the Casa and my clients back home. To the friends that I made in Abadiânia who were also on their journeys and supported me on mine, I thank you.

And with deep appreciation, I thank the following people:

My family, my mom and my girls, who believe in me and support me through my crazy adventures. My Auntie Pauline and cousin Ric, my spiritual sounding boards.

Those who documented my story: Josef, Liz, Harry, Marcus, Jalal, Jeanette, and Rose. My dear friend Mara, without whom this book would probably never have gotten published. And those who helped her put this together, particularly Marie, Lynn, Dawn, Leah, and Kathy. And Peter for guiding me. A special mention to my dear friend Mark who has supported me from the beginning of my journey.

My dear friend Aedan for her beautiful music to accompany me. Robert of the Conscious Life Expo and Ken of the New Living Expo for creating a forum for me. And especially to my spiritual group and friends who have attended, volunteered, and supported me at my events.

Susan, Chantal, and Suzy for getting me there.

Sean "Spikey" for being there.

And of course Josef, who I hope will always be there...

But most of all, my deep gratitude to the profound and miraculous

Medium João

And to the divine and beautiful spirits who work with him.

And to God, for through God all things are possible....

As a small token of my appreciation, I dedicate a portion of the proceeds from this book to the Casa de Dom Inácio for the continuation of the amazing work they do.

The Triangle

THE TRIANGLE is a significant symbol at the Casa de Dom
Inácio. The three sides of the triangle represent Faith (Fé),
Love (Amor), and Charity (Caridade). There are three wooden
triangles at the Casa. One is inside the Great Hall and the others
are along outer walls. Photos, prayers, and healing petitions placed
inside the triangle are given to the Entity for his blessing. A person
may also pray at the triangle. Often this is done by bowing one's
forehead in the center and placing one's arms along the sides of the
triangle.

Feedback

Tell me your story!

As you have read this book and allowed your thoughts to connect with John of God and the spirits of the Casa, you have already made the connection. Your healing has already begun. Expect miracles to appear in your life. Not just physical health but emotional well-being, a sense of peace, love, and happiness. Expect a more prosperous, wonderful life as your desires manifest more easily. Try consciously asking for what you want. The spirits are waiting to assist you. Then as these things come to pass, don't forget to thank them.

I would love to hear your personal experiences as you connect with this energy. Please write and let me know what resonated with you and what positive changes happen in your life. I may use your feedback on my website or in other media, so in writing to me you are giving your permission to use your story and comments unless you include in your correspondence that you do not want it published. I cannot promise to respond personally to all your emails but I do review my own email. All email addresses on my healing list travel with me on my journeys and receive blessings. I look forward to hearing from you.

Gail Thackray

Please email me at: feedback@GailThackray.com

About the Author

GAIL THACKRAY was raised in Yorkshire, England and prides herself on having kept her English down-to-earth sensibility. Her life changed at age forty when she discovered she was a medium and able to talk to spirits on the other side. Helping others connect to Source and to develop their own natural psychic abilities is her passion. Gail lectures at events worldwide, doing live appearances as a healer, medium, and educator. When at home in Los Angeles, she writes, lectures, and teaches about mediumship, healing, animal communication, manifesting, and other aspects of spirituality.

Gail is the host of the documentary series "Gail Thackray's Spiritual Journeys," interviewing eminent spiritual leaders and experiencing places of great spiritual and supernatural significance. Traveling the world, Gail leads groups to see John of God in Brazil as well as on other spiritual adventures. Gail's mission is to help people experience alignment with Divine Source and to bring this powerful energy into their own lives.

To find out how you can accompany Gail on one of her journeys or to learn more about her books, documentary series, and live events, please visit her website:

www.GailThackray.com